internet
protect
your kids

Keep your children safe from
the dark side of technology

internet protect your kids

your kids

Keep your children safe from
the dark side of technology

stephen arterburn
roger marsh

Published by
THOMAS NELSON
Since 1798

www.thomasnelson.com

INTERNET PROTECT YOUR KIDS

Copyright © 2007 by Stephen Arterburn and Roger Marsh.

Published by Integrity Publishers, a division of Thomas Nelson, Inc., PO Box 141000, Nashville, Tennessee 37214.

Published in association with the literary agency of WordServe Literary Group, 10152 S. Knoll Circle, Highlands Ranch, Colorado, 80130.

Unless otherwise indicated, Scripture quotations are taken from The New King James Version ®. Copyright © 1982 by Thomas Nelson, Inc. Used by permission. All rights reserved.

Cover Design: Scott Lee Designs
Cover Photo: Steve Gardner, PixelWorks Studio, Inc., shootpw.com
Interior Design: Teresa Billingsley

Library of Congress Cataloging-in-Publication Data

Arterburn, Stephen, 1953-

   Internet protect your kids : keep your children safe from the dark side of technology / by Stephen Arterburn and Roger Marsh.

      p. cm.

   Summary: "Easy lessons to teach parents how to monitor their kids' activity online"—Provided by publisher.

   ISBN-13: 978-1-59145-571-4 (tradepaper)

   ISBN-10: 1-59145-571-5 (tradepaper)

1. Internet and children—United States. 2. Computer crimes—United States—Prevention. 3. Internet—Safety measures. I. Marsh, Roger. II. Title.

   HQ784.I58A77 2007

   004.67'80289—dc22

2006033660

Printed in the United States of America
07 08 09 10 11 RRD 9 8 7 6 5 4 3 2 1

CONTENTS

FOREWORD

On December 26, 2004, my family and I watched the TV in shock as the Asian Tsunami killed thousands of people and devastated the lives of millions more. In the hours that followed after the storm hit, many of the television news reports alternated between showing footage of the incredibly tranquil water and beauty of the tropical paradise in Thailand right *before* the worst storm recorded in modern history hit . . . and the devastation that was left in its wake after the fact. As we sat in our safe, warm, home we kept asking "How could this happen? Weren't there any signs to let them know of this impending disaster?"

I love the ocean. I live near the Pacific. Our family vacations at the ocean. We swim, we surf, and frankly, we love to have fun in the ocean. However, sometimes we underestimate the power of the water we call our friend. It is simply too vast for us to understand completely – but that doesn't keep us from wanting to use it just the same.

In many ways, the World Wide Web is a great deal like my experience with the ocean. I love the Internet and use it every day. I can read devotionals and inspiration at the touch of a button. Today, in 2 minutes I looked up the 10-day weather forecast for a city I am flying to this week. Information is literally at our fingertips about health and research and improving our family life. I even did some marriage counseling today via e-mail. The Web is an amazing invention. However, as Roger and Steve will tell you in this book, it is also scary and dangerous. It can fuel the pain of addiction or unhealthy lifestyle choices that can wind up hitting our kids' lives with the same force as a Tsunami. And unfortunately for us as parents, sometimes the unwise choices our kids make about their relationship with the Internet go unnoticed, even after the Tsunami of negativity hits their lives.

If you are anything like me, you will use and enjoy the Web. But the Internet means much more to your kids. They *live* by it. They will spend more hours in a week on the Internet than watching TV. I was reminded of that fact not too long ago when my daughter was doing a research paper and was looking for medical information. When I suggested she could use some of our old Encyclopedias and a medical book written three years ago, all I got back from her was a blank stare. Why would she look at old books, when you could go online for the latest information? I forgot for a moment that it is a new world of communication and information and it will *never* go back.

My 88-year-old dad doesn't use or trust ATM's, but that doesn't mean I will not use them. I know some adults don't use the Internet but that doesn't mean that it will not be the number one way your kids will communicate and get information. With this thought in mind, we must become students of the Internet and learn how to protect our kids from the dangers of traveling in Cyberspace.

Would you allow a sexual predator to baby-sit your kids? Of course not! But each day, literally thousands of enemies of children prowl the Internet looking for vulnerable kids to prey upon. And that's just one area where the kids are at risk each time they go online. The dark side of the Internet is very dark. And I believe every parent must learn the basics of Internet protection. We can't leave it up to our kids, the schools, or even the church.

Before our children could walk we were preparing them to live near the ocean. They're in college now, but even so we *still* remind them of the dangers of riptides and other perils of the sea. Today we must do the same with the Internet. We can't expect our kids to be wise enough or mature enough to handle the Internet without our watchful eyes and helpful instruction.

This generation of kids needs loving and firm leadership from their parents on this topic. That's why I am ecstatic that you are holding this book in your hands. Both Roger Marsh and Steve Arterburn are two of my closest friends and partners in the battle for kids' souls. They are experts in their field of work. They live what they write and speak about and just as important, they care deeply for your family. Roger is the producer of the daily HomeWord broadcasts. He is one of the most talented and gifted people I have ever met. I marvel at his ability to communicate. Steve and I have been close friends for over 20 years. Frankly, I have never met a finer communicator with more insight than Steve. I have read this book cover to cover. My life and approach to the Internet will be forever changed and forever made better because of their writing.

Jim Burns, Ph.D.
President, HomeWord
Author of *Creating An Intimate Marriage*

INTRODUCTION

Sara didn't live too far from the park where her soccer team played, so she usually rode her bike or walked home whenever practice or a game was over.

On this particular night, she was walking, not really paying attention to what was going on around her. But when she heard the footsteps, her heart skipped a beat.

What was that noise? she wondered. "Come on, Sara," she said to herself under her breath. "This is the safest street in the world. No one's going to hurt you here."

She hurried home anyway, then raced upstairs and logged on. The "buddy list" for her screen name, HisGirl7, appeared on the screen. She noticed that several of her "buddies" were also online, including TheMan23. He was a new friend she had made only a couple of days ago, but she had fun chatting with him so she sent him an instant message.

HisGirl7: hey wassup?
TheMan23: hey yourself J
HisGirl7: omg i thot sum weirdo was following me home today
TheMan23: u watch too many chick flix J lol i thought u lived in a safe place
HisGirl7: yeah i do except for my dork neighbor lol
TheMan23: maybe it wuz one of his loser friends
HisGirl7: not even
TheMan23: what if some psycho dude got ur name. have u ever given it online?
HisGirl7: no wayyyyyyyy!!!!!!! i'm not stupid
TheMan23: did u have soccer today?
HisGirl7: yeah we had a game we won but I played pretty sucky
TheMan23: did you score?

HisGirl7: no—im the goalie J
TheMan23: my bad lol. ur on all-stars, right?
HisGirl7: yay yay—we are the east valley galaxy baby!!!!!
TheMan23: thatz so kewl
HisGirl7: gtg im grounded from IM and my parents just got home. ttfn

Sara quickly signed off and headed downstairs to greet her parents. Meanwhile, TheMan23 went to the member menu to search for HisGirl7's profile. When it came up on the screen, he quickly printed it out.

He learned that HisGirl7 was Sara Jackson. She lived in Colorado and was born January 3. She would be fourteen on her next birthday. She was an eighth-grader at the local middle school. Her hobbies included soccer (obviously), playing the saxophone, and hanging out with her friends. She was also a leader in her church's junior high youth group.

This wasn't the first time TheMan23 "just happened to be online" when Sara got home from soccer. Even though he had only been her online friend for about a week, she had already told him plenty about herself during their chats. He knew she usually logged on around 5 p.m. and always had to log off just before 6:30 when her parents got home from work. She had been talking nonstop about making the soccer all-stars this year, and he used an online search engine to show him where the East Valley region was. It even showed him the exact location of the park where Sara played and what it really looked like.

TheMan23 now had enough information to find her. Even though he lived in a different state, he just needed to know when her next game was . . . and he would find that out from her during tomorrow's online chat.

Sara felt it was best not to tell her mom and dad about the footsteps she thought she'd heard on her way home. They'd probably just wig out anyway, she figured. She certainly didn't want to make a scene. Being an only child, Sara always felt like her parents were overprotective, so she didn't want to lose what little independence she had after school. And a loss of privileges could spell the end of her online friendships altogether.

The day arrived for Sara's next soccer all-stars game. She was understandably excited, but also felt a little nervous at the same time, as if someone were watching her. It was the same feeling she'd had a couple of days before when she heard the footsteps while walking home.

She noticed a man along the near sideline who didn't look like any of the dads of the other girls on her team. In fact, this guy just didn't seem like he was part of the group at all. But it was all-stars, so she still wasn't quite sure which parents went with which of her teammates. And since he didn't look too scary, Sara shrugged it off, took her place in goal, and the game began.

The man spotted the East Valley goalkeeper straight away and knew he had found his target. He watched from the sideline, easily chatting up the other parents as the game wore on. Once the final whistle blew, the stranger offered a few words of congratulations to Sara's coach and then waited for her to leave the field. Work obligations had kept both of her parents from attending the game, but, as always, Sara didn't mind the walk home. Her team had won, after all. She was so happy about the outcome she didn't notice that the stranger from the soccer field was following her just a few steps behind. Once he saw where she lived, he quickly returned to the park to get his car.

Rather than heading straight over to Sara's house, the stranger decided instead to drive to a nearby fast-food place for something to eat. He would have plenty of time to get to know Sara much better later in the day . . .

Chapter 1

THE INTERNET: A WAY OF LIFE FOR OUR KIDS

"My son just got an A on a history project for his fourth-grade class—and he did all the research online."

"It seems like my kids spend all of their free time on MySpace. It's like they're addicted to it. Are they?"

The Internet can seem like a mystery to adults, yet most kids feel right at home there. For some, it's a helpful tool for research. For others, it's the place to make new friends and socialize.

"My friends and I like gaming online. It's pretty cool to play World of Warcraft with thousands of other kids all over the world at the same time."

"When I was eleven I got this e-mail that looked like it was from one of my friends . . . but it turned out to be a link to a porno Web site. It was no big deal, I guess."

Of course you want your kids to have a normal childhood, and the new "normal" for children involves using the Internet—a lot. But you're an involved parent, so you want to make sure you know how to make the Internet safe, educational, and yet still fun for your kids. As well you should.

"One time I met this guy in a chat room, and it seemed like we were getting along really well. So when he asked me out, I thought it would be pretty cool, you know, to go on a date with a 'mystery guy' I had never met in person before."

Your kids are part of a generation that craves community and relationship, and thinks it can find both on the Internet. So how do you let them explore without putting them in harm's way?

THE NEW "NORMAL"

You're reading this right now because you're looking for answers. Your deepest fears are that you don't really know what your kids are doing online. You're concerned they'll get hurt by their actions. And you're afraid that if they do wind up in a bad situation, you won't know how to help them.

Fortunately, there are answers to your questions about Internet safety. It *is* possible for your children to have a safe and positive Internet experience. All it takes is a parent like you who is willing to *regroup, retrain,* and *redeem.*

"But all my friends are on MySpace, Mom. Why can't I have my own profile?" If that sounded like some kind of secret code to you, you're not alone. Social networking Web sites like MySpace.com have become the place where kids like to hang out online, often because there are supposedly no parents there.

In just a few short years, the Internet has gone from a school luxury to a social necessity for kids. There are twenty-four million kids ages twelve to seventeen in the United States, and 87 percent of them use the Internet regularly—with 44 percent of them going online *every day.*[1]

Your kids just want to be doing what all the other kids their age are doing. They're spending hours each day on the Internet. They instant message (IM) their friends about their homework while they're downloading music from iTunes. They blog on MySpace while they play *World of Warcraft* online with other players from all over the world, most of whom they'll never ever actually meet in person.

On the surface, those might seem like "normal kid" activities. But there's a dark side to modern technology as well. According to Family Safe Media, the largest consumer group of Internet pornography is boys ages twelve to seventeen. The average age of a child viewing porn online for the first time is eleven.[2] One in three teenagers has unwillingly encountered pornography within the past year. During that same time period, 17 percent of all children were exposed to such material through an e-mail or instant message.[3] And the number of cases of "cyberbullying" continues to grow at an astonishing rate.

You probably turned to this book because you're confused, scared, concerned, and uncertain. But what exactly are you so afraid of? After all, bringing a computer into the home was most likely *your* idea. You used one at work every day and no one ever got hurt. You sent a few e-mails, booked a vacation or two, checked the news headlines, picked up a few priceless treasures on eBay . . . so, you figured, how could it possibly be a bad thing to open up these possibilities to your family? And in many ways, you were right. Having a computer in the house has likely made life easier for everyone.

When your kids first went online at home, you probably felt you were doing a pretty good job of making sure the Internet was a safe place for them. But then they began e-mailing their friends all the time. Then the IMs started. Pretty soon, they were gaming online. And then MySpace came out of nowhere. Before you knew it, your kids were the online experts . . . and now you've been left with the feeling that you don't even know *who* your kids are anymore—all while your eight-year-old wants to know why he can't have his own online profile.

A Sneaking Suspicion

Welcome to the MySpace Generation, also known as "Generation @." It may seem like it's made up of some of the nicest, most responsible kids you've ever met—and they probably are. The only difference between this generation and those that have gone before it is the size and influence of its peer group.

It used to be that truly involved parents would get to know as many of the peer influencers as they could in their child's life, whether through school activities, church groups, or extracurriculars like sports, debate team, or the arts. These days, however, the peer group a child has can number in the *millions*, and all because of the influence of the Internet and modern technology.

The statistics don't give you much confidence. Sixty-two percent of parents who have "online teens" believe their kids are viewing things on the Internet that they wouldn't approve of.[4] That fact may sadden you, but deep down you might not be all that surprised. And maybe that's because the exact same percentage of those online teens agree that, yes, most kids *are* looking at Web sites and other material on the Internet that their parents wouldn't let them see if they knew they were doing it.[5]

So you picked up a book like this one. You hope it will help you protect your kids from sexual predators, gambling, pornography, drug abuse, and any other of the myriad of deviant behaviors that seem to thrive online. But still, you have your doubts.

You've heard about the nice teenage girl from a good family who made a few new friends online—one of whom was actually a much older sexual predator who enticed her into a rendezvous that ended up costing her life. You wonder if the same thing might happen to *your* daughter—and, naturally, you worry. Maybe *panic* is a better word for it. It's that empty feeling you have inside after talking with your thirteen-year-old son, who assures you that all the time he spends online is only with his friends . . . but you know deep down that he's one step away from developing a drug habit, and that he's getting his drugs online.

Obviously, you want to keep your kids safe from sexual predators online. You want to keep them drug-free. You don't want them using the Internet to "hook up" with friends for sex, but you're afraid they will anyway.

That fear has grown stronger still since your best friend at church tearfully told you that her fifteen-year-old daughter had been having sex with a couple of different guys from the youth group. She found out that they were arranging their "hookups" online, and she had no idea that anything was wrong until her daughter tested positive for a sexually transmitted disease.

LIKE IT OR NOT, IT'S HERE

True, these things can happen. The Internet can be a scary place. But that doesn't mean that you have to live in fear of it. All you need is the desire to *regroup* with the other parents in your circle of influence . . . and then purpose to *retrain* your parenting style to include a more proactive approach to online safety . . . in order to *redeem* the relationship with your children that they want and need from you.

You *can* do this! You're probably the kind of parent who was actively involved in the lives of your children as they grew up. Soccer practice, Girl Scouts, math homework, church camp . . . whatever it was, you were there, making sure your kids had every opportunity to make good friends, get good grades, and take part in the kinds of activities they enjoy. You were involved without intruding, supportive without smothering. And your kids really seemed to enjoy the connection they shared with you.

They talked to you about everything because your presence in their lives made them feel safe, secure, and loved. And it still does. Only now the rules have changed. All children want and need that sense of community and connection, but now they're finding it—or at least something that feels a lot like it—on the Internet. Because whether they admit it or not, *that's* the primary reason that 87 percent of all teenagers go online each day.

So maybe that's the real reason why you picked up this book. Because you care so much about your kids that you'll do *anything* to protect them, even if it means sticking your nose in their business and finding out what they do and where they go online. Or swallowing your pride a little and asking your kids about how MySpace works, or why they would want to be friends online with a girl whose profile page is as pornographic as any so-called "adult" movie out there.

You may never have imagined yourself confronting your son about whether or not he has ever placed a bet online. Or asking your daughter how many unsolicited pornographic pop-up advertisements she had to delete from her laptop last week. Those aren't easy questions to ask, but they're part of an ongoing dialog you will need to establish and maintain to keep your kids safe online.

You don't have to be afraid of the Internet or this MySpace Generation. Make your peace with the reality that the Internet is here to stay, and then equip yourself with the tools you need to *Internet Protect Your Kids!*

Chapter 2

THE INTERNET PLAYGROUND: WHY KIDS SPEND SO MUCH TIME ONLINE

In May 2006, Pennsylvania congressman Michael G. Fitzpatrick introduced legislation in the House of Representatives that would make it illegal for minors to access social networking sites such as MySpace and Facebook. As part of an effort to keep underage children from online predators and from viewing pornographic images, the proposed bill would also ban libraries from making such access possible. Fitzpatrick's "Deleting Online Predators Act of 2006" would mandate the creation of an eight-member advisory board to the Federal Communications Commission, in addition to a government-sponsored and operated Web site warning parents about the dangers of social networking sites.[1]

Katherine Lester was in love.

This was no schoolgirl crush. She had met the man of her dreams and was prepared to travel half a world away from her

Michigan home to be with him. Never mind the fact that Katherine was a sixteen-year-old honor student and her "dream love" was a twenty-five-year-old man from Jericho, Israel, on the West Bank. Katherine somehow convinced her mother to drive her to the airport, where she boarded a plane for Amman, Jordan. It was there, however, where U.S. authorities, on a tip from the FBI, were able to meet up with Katherine and persuade her to return home before the situation got any worse.

The young girl met her "true love" on MySpace.com. She almost met an uncertain fate with a man she barely knew in a country that's not exactly a haven for Americans these days. So why would a bright, intelligent young girl put herself in harm's way over a guy she met on a social networking Web site? Perhaps the bigger question is, What exactly *is* MySpace, and why do so many kids like using it?

KEEP THE COMPUTER OUT OF THE BEDROOM

There are several ways to *Internet Protect Your Kids*, but the most basic is to make sure the computer in your house is kept in a public place. Depending on the size and configuration of your home, an area like the living room, entertainment room, or even the kitchen should be suitable. *Under no circumstances should a child in your home have unlimited Internet access from a computer in his own bedroom—ever.*

There are too many "accidental temptations" awaiting a young child who misspells a word while doing a search for a school project, for example. Or a teenager who's savvy enough to cover his online tracks while browsing hundreds of pornographic sites. Of course, placing an Internet-connected computer in your child's room may be a mistake you've already made. According to a study by the Henry Kaiser Foundation, 31 percent of kids eight to eighteen have a computer in their bedroom, and 20 percent of those kids have Internet access in their bedrooms as well.[2] If you've already allowed this to happen, correct it—*now*!

PARENTAL CONTROLS

Keeping computers out of a child's bedroom is only half the battle. The next step is to restrict any form of online communication that was not set up with parental consent. Any e-mail or IM account created for a child's use must be established by a parent. The same holds true for establishing a profile on an SNS such as MySpace or Xanga. And for kids who split time with their parents because of a divorce, both mother and father need to establish an Internet protocol that will be in effect in *both households*. In such cases, the biological parents are responsible for establishing and enforcing these rules with their children, and stepparents *must* support their spouses in this area.

THE MYSPACE PHENOMENON

MySpace is currently the most popular social networking site on the Internet. A social networking site (SNS) is simply a place where users exchange instant messages and pictures, "chat" online about life, love, and music, and basically just hang out with each other.

The financial ramifications of hanging out on a site such as MySpace are usually nominal because the majority of SNSes are available to use free of charge. The logic behind that is the same as with network television: the larger the membership on a site, the more that site's operator can then charge advertisers in fees to place "banner ads" throughout the site. Advertisers also pay what's called a "click fee" for each time a site user clicks on their ad.

If you feel blindsided by all of these recent online meeting places, you're not alone. Terms like "MySpace" and "social networking site" didn't really start to make an impression in cyberspace until around 2001. The first few attempts to establish a foundation for this genre did not anticipate such an overwhelming response and were unable to keep up with demands. Among those early ventures was a site called Xanga, which eventually survived the rush by morphing into one of the first SNSes. Friendster was another early bird that proved the demand was high.

Then in July 2003, a couple of California twentysomethings founded "a place for friends" called MySpace.com, and the communication revolution became official. Tom Anderson and Chris DeWolfe had a vision for creating an interactive Web site where college kids could promote music that they liked. Since many of the artists behind the music were unknown and/or unsigned, they could use all the free publicity they could get—and who better to give it to them than some of their most adoring fans!

Combining their collective passion for music and knowledge of Internet technology, Anderson and DeWolfe (along with a small team of programmers) opened up MySpace to any user eighteen years of age or older. No credit card or other form of ID was required. Just set up a profile and start promoting those bands!

EXPLODING SPACE IN A SHRINKING WORLD

MySpace quickly became much more popular than Anderson and DeWolfe could have ever imagined. Both of these "tech junkies" were fascinated with all the new gadgetry that was available for Web sites—instant messaging, streaming audio and video, among others—and they began adding these features to MySpace. The site became the "it" place for the college set and for the millions of under-eighteens who also began creating profiles.

Realizing that the concept was growing in popularity among high school students, MySpace first lowered its minimum age to sixteen, then eventually to its present level of fourteen. The strategy almost immediately proved successful, as the premiere SNS became an industry unto itself.

Just how big has MySpace become? In 2005, News Corp (the parent company of 20th Century Fox) paid $580 million to purchase MySpace.com. At the time, the site had a little more than twenty million user profiles. Exactly one year later, MySpace boasted more than eighty million user profiles, and it crossed the

100 million mark shortly thereafter. At the same time, MySpace passed Google and Yahoo! to become the leading Web site in terms of "page views," recognized as the industry standard for success. It wasn't long before MySpace and Google made headlines together once again with the announcement of an arrangement whereby Google would be the exclusive search engine provider for MySpace. Total value of that deal: $900 million.

WHAT'S ALL THE ATTRACTION?

While such numbers reveal the industry clout MySpace has among its Web peers, younger users aren't heading there by the millions because it's become a money-making machine. The appeal of MySpace and other SNSes is the fact that they give *every* account holder a place to feel they belong. During the adolescent years, teens and preteens are driven by seemingly contradictory passions. They want *recognition* without being *recognized*. The need for peer acceptance is high at this age, but so is the desire to establish a personal identity. Social networking sites give teens and preteens the feeling that they can have both—to *stand out* without being *singled out*.

On the personal expression side, these online hubs offer kids the opportunity to create a completely unique page that's all about them—and no one else. Each user can set up his personal profile as equal parts info sheet, online diary, and "life" yearbook. If you've never heard the term "user-generated content" before, get used to hearing it. The under-twenty-five set *loves* to express its creativity online, and a MySpace profile provides the perfect outlet. Users can "stream" music and videos (i.e., they can watch or listen at the same time the content downloads). They can also blog (cyberslang for a "Web log," this is simply an online journal of sorts) their deepest or silliest thoughts about anything and everything. And they can post pictures—as many as they want, of whatever they want.

At the same time that they're expressing themselves, kids can get to know other people with similar interests. Sites such as MySpace, Xanga, Facebook and the like all offer teens and pre-teens a place to hang out and meet friends—usually without parental consent—that they likely would never encounter without the worldwide reach of the Web.

UNPREPARED FOR THE UNEXPECTED

Stacy seemed obsessed with creating the perfect MySpace profile. She used the coolest wallpaper for the background of her landing page. She kept a healthy assortment of her favorite music videos streaming there as well. She certainly wasn't shy when it came to the topics she liked to blog about. And there were pictures—*dozens* of pictures of this cute fourteen-year-old and her friends and family.

As far as she knew, Stacy had put together a truly "awesome" MySpace profile. She was proud of the fact that she had made the varsity cheerleading squad, even though she was only a freshman at Hoover High. Her profile included a clever countdown ticker showing the exact number of hours, minutes, and seconds till her sixteenth birthday. Many of the pictures in her profile were taken in front of her home or at her school. A few even included local landmarks from the well-known Midwestern city where she lived. Stacy craved making new friends online and even went so far as to include her cell phone number in her profile.

It was only a matter of time before a sexual predator started grooming Stacy to become his next victim. She had left far too many clues for him on her MySpace profile. Using a combination of IM, e-mail, and text messaging, he was able to arrange a meeting with her in far less time than it usually took for him to make his move.

With tens of millions of user profiles and exponentially fewer known predators online, a social networking Web site can be an extremely dangerous place for a fourteen-year-old girl like Stacy. The voyeuristic nature of the Internet means that what attracts a child to a site such as MySpace is also what can lead her into a potentially dangerous relationship online. With more than 150 million Americans using the Internet, it's safe to say that literally millions of people have direct access to a user's profile. A young boy who likes to check out other profiles, for example, might do so without realizing that he is subject to the same scrutiny and could be leaving himself open to unwanted advances from a sexual predator.

That's why, in early 2006, the operators of MySpace stepped up their efforts to heighten the level of safety afforded to each account holder. A new security staff was hired and more than

---

Monitor Cell Phone and IM Activity

Many parents are more willing to give their child a cell phone than to condone unlimited Internet access. But the reality is the two are often used in tandem. Online connections can be initiated via e-mail or IM, and then culminated on a cell phone—or vice versa. That's why it's crucial to get printed copies of your son or daughter's cell phone bills each month and actually *read them* to verify the charges are accurate. Many cell phone service providers are encouraging their customers to settle up their accounts each month online, so make sure your provider knows you expect a hard copy of your bill at the end of each billing cycle. Also, require your children to provide you with full access to their instant messaging online and text messaging on the cell phones. No access, no use.

---

100 new staffers were added to the payroll. Their job: to check various user profiles at random for content violations and potential activity from sexual predators. While this was taken as a truly encouraging sign by the industry, it also means the chances are less than one in one million that a user will get caught putting something potentially harmful or obscene in their profile. That's why it's up to *you* as a parent to play a more active role in screening what your child may or may not include in her profile on an SNS.

YOU'RE NOT THE ONLY ONE

For every kid with a MySpace profile, there's a parent who has a MySpace horror story—or so it would seem, based upon the numerous reports of sexual assaults and cyberstalkers on the Internet. In reality, the incidence of malicious behavior on SNSes is relatively small in proportion to the number of currently active account holders. Yet even one assault is too many, so it's our hope that what you'll read on the pages that follow will help you keep your son or daughter from being another statistic.

Many parents have a MySpace story that does not involve an online assault, just one that deals with the shocking discovery that their kids were using this new technology and Mom and Dad had no clue as to either what they were doing or how they were doing it. If that's you, realize that you're not the first parent to discover that your kids found a way around your "no MySpace at home" family rule. Be thankful that yours isn't a more painful story about a son who was the victim of "cyberbullying," or of the sexual predator who stalked a daughter online before meeting her in person and killing her.

Think about how you felt when you first discovered your kids were essentially creating different personalities online than the ones you were used to seeing around the house (because as we'll find out later, that's often what happens). Maybe it was a sense of betrayal from knowing your kids had lied to you—or simply remained intentionally silent—about what they were doing. Maybe you felt a gripping fear after hearing reports of sexual predators lurking online. Or maybe you really didn't have feelings one way or the other about it because your kids seemed to be enjoying using the Internet, and no one had gotten hurt—yet.

THE SECRET LIFE OF A PRETEEN

Lori was a mother of two whose husband had recently died of a massive heart attack. She found herself in a place she never could have imagined—a widow in her mid-thirties trying to be both

Mom *and* Dad to a couple of bright but headstrong preteen daughters. Madison seemed to do as good a job of coping with her father's death as a twelve-year-old could. But the loss hit her ten-year-old sister, Megan, much harder.

Megan was a bright, beautiful, and intelligent girl. She always did well in school and was active in the youth group at her church. After her dad died, Megan's grandfather and grandmother took a more active role in helping their daughter, Lori, raise the two girls. Megan's grandpa, Ted, used to say that his youngest granddaughter was "a natural born leader," but he was also insightful enough to see that Megan didn't always make the best decisions when it came to choosing friends. He had noticed that both of his granddaughters spent a lot of time online, but he trusted that they were using the Internet safely. "Besides," he figured, "Lori seems to have a good connection with them." And yet he had a nagging suspicion that they might be heading for trouble online.

Ted was the manager of a firm that often contracted business with local government agencies. As a result, a tremendous amount of sensitive information was often transmitted via e-mail between Ted's firm and its clients. To provide the company with an extra measure of accountability should any employee decide to engage in a little "business on the side" with one of those clients, Ted began receiving e-mail reports that listed all the online activity for each employee in the firm for that day.

The idea of monitoring e-mail, instant messaging, and Internet browsing struck a nerve with Ted. He installed the same software on every computer in his home, where Lori, Madison, and Megan were now living. At first, Lori was resigned to just let her girls "do their thing" online while she remained clueless. But Ted continued to encourage his daughter to keep up with her girls' Internet-based activities. Madison and Megan regularly carried on multiple IM conversations at once, using cyberlingo that sounded like a foreign language to Lori. It took her several months before she could really keep up and know what her daughters were talking about with their friends online.

Once she felt she was up to speed, however, Lori went to work. The monitoring software gave her a record of each Web site her daughters visited. It also provided her with records of each e-mail and IM conversation. By the time Lori began to do her homework, Madison was fourteen and the subject matter of her correspondence was fairly typical for a girl her age: boys, dating, teachers, music, *more* boys. But Lori was growing more concerned about Megan. Although the youngest daughter was about to turn thirteen, she was already involved in some drug dealing.

Megan earned money performing a service known in the drug trade as "muling." A dealer would set up a "buy" with a customer, then arrange for Megan to be his "mule." She would pick up the drugs, deliver them to the client, get the cash from the client, and then "mule" the money back to the dealer. Megan never knew the identity of either the dealer or the user; she would simply wait for one of her other contacts in the trade to send her an IM with the cell number of a dealer who'd be calling her the next day. If she saw that number come up on the caller ID on her own cell phone, Megan was to answer the call and get the pickup and drop-off instructions from the dealer. Then she would make the score and IM back to her contact that the deal was complete.

Lori was shocked to discover Megan's secret life. She knew that confronting Megan would be a risk, but doing nothing would be even riskier. So, backed by the support of her parents, Lori confronted Megan about her drug trafficking. At first she denied it, but eventually she admitted to everything she had done. She told her mom that she had never used the drugs she was selling, but that she liked the money she was making as a "mule" and didn't think it was a big deal for her to continue. That opinion changed after Lori explained the legal reality of the situation, with some helpful statistics and information from her father. For both Megan and Lori, it was a serious wake-up call about how dangerous a little social networking online can become.

INVOLVED BUT NOT CONNECTED

It wasn't easy for Ted to trust his gut that one of his granddaughters might be using the Internet to get into serious trouble. And it was a courageous if not painful step for Lori to confront her daughter with the reality that she was in trouble with the law for the trafficking of illegal drugs. How could something like this happen to a parent who felt she was doing all she could to keep up with her children?

You may be asking a similar question. Like most parents today, you've probably gone overboard to make sure you stayed involved in your kids' lives. You've arranged your work schedules to be more available to your kids than your own parents *ever* were for you. You've been a coach and a referee. You've driven countless hours and thousands of miles to ballet recitals and church youth-group broomball nights at the local ice skating rink at 2 a.m. You've gone above and beyond the call of duty to make your house a place where your kids and their friends like to hang out. But now you're beginning to wonder how the Internet could have become such a huge part of the lives of your children *without* you really noticing it.

The subtle change typically begins with your kids wanting to spend more and more of their time online and less time with family. They'll put in a full day at school, followed by a couple of hours of an extracurricular activity like band or soccer, and then rush home to the computer and immediately go online. There, they'll check their MySpace profile, blog about something on their mind, and then start IMing their friends about the day's events.

To be fair, there are many kids who *do* take it upon themselves to use every precaution available to protect themselves from predators. But all the safety nets in the world won't change the fact that our kids have entered into this new realm without us, and they seem perfectly content to keep things that way.

So here we are: The parents who worked so hard to build an unbreakable bond with our children—or so we thought—are now confronted with the feeling that our connection was somehow falsified. It's as if our kids saved their *real* thoughts, feelings, hopes, and dreams for their MySpace friends.

What Can Parents Do?

At this point we have a couple of options available to us. We can choose to rip the computer out of the wall and forbid our kids to ever go online at home again—which will assuredly make them even more determined to find their way back online *without* parental supervision or involvement. Or we can have a good sulk . . . and then decide to look as objectively as we can at this new "community" our kids are finding online. It's a world that isn't all *bad*, but the key is helping our children recognize that there are parts of it that aren't all that *good* either.

What you're reading right now is the result of many hours of researching and soul-searching by a couple of concerned dads on behalf of millions of other parents and grandparents. Like you, we want to protect our kids from the dangers of the virtual life while affirming them in their quest to be recognized without standing out for the wrong reasons. Of course, that's not always an easy task, especially when your kids are smart enough to outsmart you online!

You know the drill: Mom and Dad establish a family rule; Son and Daughter do everything they can to find a way *around* it. It's not going to be any different when you start establishing your family's Internet Usage Agreement, if you don't already have one in place. (Check Appendix A to see HomeWord's sample Internet Usage Agreement.) If your kids find that the house rules are too confining, they're bound to look for *somewhere else* to go online, like maybe their best friend's house.

Fortunately, there is a way you can extend your reach in this area. *Do not* let your children access the Internet from computers outside your home without the supervision of adults who understand and support your values. This might seem easier said than done, but once you start sharing your own views on Internet safety with other parents, you'll be pleasantly surprised to discover most parents are of the same opinion.

(Note: If this request leads to resistance from other parents, use the opportunity to either enroll them in a support system providing Internet safety for your kids or consider the reasons you're friends with these people in the first place.)

It's a fact that our children need to have lives of their own. They need to cultivate their own interests and friends, and social networking sites such as MySpace give them a place to do that without parental interference. We get that.

But the goal of effective parenting is not to raise "good kids" but responsible adults. Any involvement we as parents have in using teen-oriented SNSes needs to stem from a desire to truly help our kids reach that goal. Don't set up a MySpace profile to relive the glory days of your youth. Your kids don't need you to be their friend; they need you to be their *parent.*

With that in mind, let's get ready to enter this new dimension of parenting. Whether you're handy with a mouse and a browser, or you'd consider yourself to be a complete "cyberidiot," the tools in this book will help you understand how virtual communication has become the new reality. You can help make it an enjoyable and beneficial experience for your children as you protect them from its potential dangers as well.

∼

Internet Protect Your Kids from Internet Overuse and Abuse by:

1. Keeping the computer in your home in a public place.
2. Setting up any profiles, e-mail, or IM accounts they may use.

3. Reading the printed copies of their cell phone bills each month to verify accuracy.
4. Requiring full access to instant messaging online and text messaging on cell phones.
5. Prohibiting access to the Internet from computers outside your home.

Chapter 3

UNDERSTANDING THE MINDSET OF ONLINE SEXUAL PREDATORS

When a boy reaches his fifteenth birthday he can find himself dealing with several conflicting emotions. Jason was no exception. Like many kids his age, he was longing for acceptance and recognition without standing out for any reason that might be considered "not cool" by his peers. As a result, he tended to shy away from the social scene that he desperately wanted to explore, which meant he didn't have a lot of friends.

His parents hoped that giving him his own laptop computer would help to change that. They encouraged him to surf the Internet, to explore the various social networking sites the other kids at school were using. So he did . . . and it didn't take long before Jason had collected a number of online friends.

Of all the kids he had become Internet buddies with, Kim was one of his favorites. She was sixteen, and, judging from the pictures in her profile, she was the kind of girl Jason would like to date—cute, athletic, and fun. They met in a chat room (an online gathering place where people of similar interests meet) with a large group of other kids who were discussing their favorite kind of music, ska (sort of a hybrid of punk, reggae, and jazz). Soon they had moved to "private" chat-room conversations, which eventually led to the exchanging of cell phone numbers and nonstop text messaging at seemingly all hours of the day.

Jason felt he had gotten to know Kim well enough to get up the nerve to ask her out, so he sent her a text message asking if he could call her at home sometime. He was a bit apprehensive about how she would respond, but her reply sent his heart racing: "u don't have 2 call me. Y don't we meet @ the mall parking lot Friday night @ 6?"

"Yes!" Jason shouted. This was going to be the best night of his young life.

The mall wasn't too far from his home, so Jason decided to walk there. He sent Kim a couple of text messages along the way, telling her how he couldn't wait to meet her in person. When he arrived at the mall, he noticed he was a few minutes early, so he waited patiently for his dream girl to arrive.

Jason was lost in his thoughts of Kim when a man in a late-model minivan pulled up alongside him and rolled down his window.

"You must be Jason," the man said.

"Yeah, that's me," Jason replied.

"Hi, Jason. I'm Kim's father," the man continued. "She's running a little behind schedule—you know how it is with girls and their makeup."

"Uh huh."

"Kim asked me to come here and pick you up so that you two can hang out at our house for a while. We've got a game room with a sixty-inch plasma TV. It's pretty cool. Hop in."

Jason was a bit confused by the change in plans, but he decided to get in the van anyway. Kim had never mentioned that her parents knew about her relationship with him. But she had never lied to him before—or so he thought.

Jason never made it to Kim's house that day because "Kim" didn't exist. Her online profile was a complete fabrication, created by the man who was claiming to be her father. In reality, he

Avoiding a Solicitation

Kids tend to be somewhat naive when they first go online. The lure of making new acquaintances can be so strong, they might not be too discriminating regarding the kinds of friends they wind up making. Teach your kids to alert you if they receive any message they perceive as hostile or threatening in nature. Assure them that they can come to you anytime if they receive a message that makes them feel uncomfortable for any reason. Any solicitation from an unknown internet or Instant Messaging source should automatically be discarded without being opened (i.e., placed in a junk folder with the sender permanently blocked).

was a convicted sex offender who was on parole for a number of sexual assaults committed against minors. He had spent the past several months grooming Jason to become his next victim. And now the boy had fallen into his trap just as planned.

The man sexually assaulted Jason repeatedly over the next several days. They drove south away from the boy's home in the Pacific Northwest toward the Mexican border. Jason was scared, hungry, and embarrassed. His cell phone was still fully charged, but his kidnapper told him he'd be killed if he even thought about trying to call for help.

A couple of days into their journey, the pair stopped in a small town in Nevada and checked into a local motel. While his captor slept, Jason mustered the courage to text message his father and tell him what had happened. Jason's dad immediately took action and called local authorities to launch a manhunt for his son. In the days that passed, the boy and his father communicated via text messaging whenever Jason had a chance to send a note with new information of his whereabouts. By the time the kidnapper and the boy had reached Galveston, Texas, state authorities and the border patrol were ready to intervene. Jason was rescued and reunited with his parents. The sexual predator was taken into custody once again.

SEXUAL PREDATORS ONLINE

It's no exaggeration to say that the Internet has become a breeding ground for sexually deviant behavior. As the popularity of social networking sites has increased, so has the number of reports of sexual predators using the Internet to find new victims. Worse still, a March 2006 survey from the National Center for Missing and Exploited Children found that 14 percent of online teens have actually had a face-to-face encounter with someone they had previously only known online—meaning the risk of assault for those kids is significantly higher.[1]

Keep a Record

If your child begins receiving repeated correspondence from someone you feel might be a cyberbully, cyberstalker, or sexual predator, create a "paper trail" of any correspondence this person has with your child. Save e-mails and IMs from the perpetrator on your computer, and be sure to print out backup copies of the exchanges as well.

Remember that a sexual predator will be less likely to use "flame mail" (hostile or malicious messages) because his motive is to try to befriend, not offend his intended victim. In fact, many times a predator could be grooming your child from a recognizable e-mail or IM address because the perpetrator has hijacked that friend's system as well. Both of these factors mean parents must pry deeper than just searching for unsolicited, insulting communication.

One in seven children who use the Internet regularly report receiving some kind of sexually suggestive remark via e-mail, IM, or text-messaging from someone they don't know.[2] And as the number of kids who go online increases, chances are those odds will increase as well.

Clearly, the presence of online sexual predators is becoming more common. Some agencies estimate that as many as fifty thousand sexual predators might be online on the most popular SNSes at any time. When you consider the fact that there are literally millions of users visiting these sites each month, the chances of your son or daughter being attacked by an online predator might seem fairly small. But the reality is that it only takes *one* sexual predator to put your child at risk.

Federal, state, and local law enforcement agencies have stepped up efforts to track down and prosecute these criminals in recent months. Most of the major news networks have captured an online sting operation on video and broadcast the results to a national television audience. These dragnets give parents a certain measure of hope that something is being done to win the war against the sexual predators who might be stalking the Internet for kids like ours.

Sadly, we must remember that the majority of these traps are set based on fictitious online profiles. The sobering truth of the matter is that *real kids* are falling victim to the advances of perpetrators they thought were just other friends online. And once a sexual predator is able to convince his victim to meet with him face-to-face—away from the TV news cameras and members of law enforcement—another teen or preteen becomes little more than another statistic in the coroner's office.

It's difficult for most of us to comprehend how a person is morally able to lure innocent adolescents into such a perverse, twisted game. And yet, as parents, our best defense can often be a knowledge of these criminals' psyche. What exactly is going on inside the mind of an online sexual predator? And how can we protect our kids from his advances?

THE MINDSET OF A SEXUAL PREDATOR

To understand the thought process of a sexual predator, kids and parents *must* understand that these individuals *do not* view their sexual tendencies as abnormal. On the contrary, most perpetrators think of their desires as perfectly natural. In their reality, they see themselves as liberators helping children "enjoy the bond" of sexual intimacy between an adult and a child.

With that mindset as his basis, the online sexual predator starts looking for a child to "recruit." The Internet provides a perpetrator with literally tens of millions of potential candidates, and once one is located, the "grooming" process begins. Jason, whom you just read about, was groomed by a predator to begin building what he thought was a trusting relationship with a teenage girl. The deeper the friendship became, the easier it was for Jason to share some of his deepest thoughts, feelings and secrets—exactly what a predator is looking for in hopes of gaining his victim's complete trust.

Not only does the Internet provide a sexual predator with a pool of new potential victims from which to draw, it also offers the support he needs to continue this lifestyle. Now, who in their right mind would actually *support* such a sexually perverse lifestyle? Other sexual predators, of course. The online community offers literally hundreds of Web sites and chat rooms where predators will actually talk shop with other perpetrators. What these individuals chat about online is not suitable for printing here, but suffice it to say that the topic of conversation includes how to fit into the mainstream while feeding their lust for sexual encounters with young children.

In reality, there's a miniscule chance that your underage children will ever wind up modeling for a kiddie porn site. However, the fact that sites like these even exist is a clear warning to parents that there *are* individuals online who are looking for kids to victimize. And what better place to begin their search than on a social networking site teeming with teens and preteens?

A FATHER'S HEARTACHE
Just one thought from Ron about his daughter, Jenny, and a tear comes to his eye. She was a bright, likable girl who had plenty of friends at school and church. How she wound up losing her life not even sixteen years after it started is difficult for him to comprehend.

Nothing Personal in Public

Kids often don't think of the Internet as a public domain. To them, it's little more than an extension of their home computer. Train your children to remember that everything they do, every word they write, and every picture they post online is in full view of everyone in the world with Internet access. Do not let your children put any incriminating material in full public view on any social networking site. This includes pictures of your family, snapshots of your house, and any sensitive information such as home phone number, address, or personal e-mail and Web site access information.

As part of the process of protecting your kids online, there are two important points to remember:

1. The cyberstalker will never have a legitimate purpose for wanting to chat online with your children, let alone arrange a face-to-face meeting. If your son tells you that he's met someone online, for instance, and this new friend seems oddly persistent in his insistence that they get together to meet, there's a good chance you have a cyberstalker on your hands—so take action!

2. If you allow your children to use a real-life picture of themselves on the landing page of their social networking site or as part of their IM profile, you have given a sexual predator all the reason he needs to want to pursue your child as his next victim. Do not let that happen!

It wasn't that long ago that she set up her MySpace profile. Seemed like most of her friends already had one, and so her parents didn't see any harm in letting her have one as well. Initially, she did what most kids do on MySpace—posted pictures, pushed music, blogged, commented, and posted bulletins with friends. But she noticed she was receiving special attention from one friend in particular. The IMing began shortly after they met online. Soon the computer activity moved to regular phoning back and forth. A face-to-face meeting was inevitable, and Jenny looked forward to it with great anticipation. But the night of her "dream rendezvous" turned out to be a nightmare.

Based on what she'd been told, Jenny thought her online beau was a fellow teenager, but he turned out to be much older.

And when he met her that fateful evening, he was not alone. Seems he wanted some of *his* friends to meet Jenny as well. They sexually assaulted her repeatedly, and when the ordeal was over, Jenny was left to deal with more than just the physical bruises. She had emotional and spiritual wounds that would take much longer to heal.

Jenny tried to reach out for help, but the pain of that process turned out to be too much for her. Shortly before her sixteenth birthday, wracked with guilt and shame over what had happened to her, Jenny took her own life.

FIRST LOVE

Sexual predators are among the most notorious stalkers on the Internet. But not all obsessive behavior is considered cyberstalking, so it's helpful to know what the term means and what it doesn't. Understand that not all obsessive behavior is inherently dangerous. In fact, sometimes, it's a part of an adolescent rite of passage. For example, feelings of romantic love during adolescence may border on the compulsive, but they don't usually lead to stalking.

During adolescence, kids are trying to make relationship decisions based upon emotions that far exceed their maturity level. As a result, it's not out of the ordinary for, say, a fifteen-year-old to develop a crush on a member of the opposite sex that seems like true love that will last forever. Should they decide, then, that the best way to show this love is through sending seventy-five "I love you" IMs a day, that's obsessive—but it's probably not stalking. (Not unless it's done after the recipient has already expressed annoyance at this.) Sometimes we call this "puppy love," but we're wise to remember that puppy love is very real to puppies. Most kids outgrow this phase, but some have a more difficult time moving through it than others.

Contrast that powerful, teenage infatuation with the prototypical cyberstalker's actions. The perpetrator is an adult who is considerably older than his intended victim. His methods may include the *malicious, premeditated, unrelenting* pursuit of a person online in hopes of one day meeting her or him in person—usually alone.

The cyberstalker seldom acts impulsively. His grooming process involves methodical and strategically planned encounters with his victims. That means the more you can do to mix up your child's online routine, the less predictability for a perpetrator, making it more difficult to stalk your child.

DANGER AFTER DARK

If your kids are younger, the possibility of them being victimized by a sexual predator online is greatly reduced. The reason is that many sexual predators are actually working professionals. During the day they're really not at liberty to browse the Internet looking for victims. They save that activity for later in the evening or night. This naturally puts teens and preteens at a significantly greater risk of exposure to a sexual predator. That being the case, you can go a long way toward protecting your kids from unwanted sexual advances online by limiting the hours you allow them to use the Internet.

There are any number of reasons why an online stalker would select a victim at random and choose to make that child his next victim. None of them are legitimate. The cyberstalker tends to be obsessive, so it's safe to say he will not be easily ignored. Once he's seen that picture of your daughter or son online and decided to make your child a victim, the perpetrator will diligently and tenaciously begin his pursuit.

CYBERSTALKING CLUES CONTINUED

Another characteristic of cyberstalking is that it is *repetitive* in nature. Fourteen-year-old Danielle thought it was a little strange when her new online friend Kyle asked for her home phone number. They had only met the day before on an SNS, and their chatting didn't seem too flirty, so she didn't respond to his IM at first. When he asked again, she ignored him again . . . but then the requests turned into demands. After two weeks of his badgering her, Danielle went to her parents for help.

Cyberstalking involves repeated attempts to cause you harm and personal discomfort. An old principle in the media business says that if something happens once, it's a *fluke*. If it happens twice, it's a *coincidence*. But if it happens three times, it's a bona fide *trend*. If your child receives an IM with a hate-filled tone, he or she may be able to ignore it until the friend who sent it has a chance to cool off a bit. But if the theme continues over a period of time, you may be dealing with a cyberstalker. In fact, the laws in some states define cyberstalking as involving at least two or more incidents that follow the same, repetitive pattern.

Different states have different laws concerning the prosecution of criminals for cyberstalking. For example, in most states a person is not considered to be a "stalker" if he begins his actions by responding to an e-mail or any "flaming" (malicious online communication) your child may have initiated without being provoked.

Another aspect of cyberstalking worth considering: The law also states that the exchanges must cause some form of *distress*. So if your children are not easily shocked, they may not feel as though they're being stalked at first. Distress can take on many forms, and you'll have a difficult time proving your case against a stalker if his actions don't cause them to feel distressed in some way. Remember, however, that this can include feelings of humiliation or even experiencing an inconvenience such as having their online password stolen or noticing that their pictures from an SNS have been taken and posted elsewhere. Distress can also mean that the person's actions have led your children to fear for their safety.

To be fair, the preteen and teen years are naturally an emotional time for kids. With the confluence of hormones and drama going on in their lives, it would be an understatement to say that adolescents are prone to overreacting from time to time. That said, keep in mind that most laws recognize that cyberstalking will typically cause a "reasonable person" undue distress. If your child has a history of psychological issues or has been victimized by an earlier trauma, the law may not recognize his or her claims of harassment as cyberstalking.

UNWANTED ADVANCES FOR UNKNOWN REASONS

What many kids fail to realize about cyberstalkers is that the perpetrator has decided that you owe him something. He has a personal vendetta against his victims. In other words, he wants revenge for something he feels that you've done to him.

A cyberstalker may see a picture of a cute girl online and decide that she reminds him of a hurtful relationship from his past. Sometimes the stalker has it in his mind that his victim has committed an unspeakable evil and it's up to him to bring about justice. Hate is a huge motivator in these cases, and it's key to remember that a cyberstalker may seek revenge for an action that may never have been committed.

The typical stalker sometimes imagines a wrong has been done to him, but occasionally, your child might be the one who started the exchange with an unprovoked attack on a friend, classmate, or casual online acquaintance. In those cases, it may be proven that, based on the legal definition of cyberstalking, the stalker had a legitimate purpose in harassing your son or daughter. Bottom line? Be sure your kids know the importance of being careful with what they say online!

SCOPING THE INDIVIDUAL

Another distinction between cyberbullying and cyberstalking involves the *target* of the attacks. Cyberstalkers always attack an *individual*. Your children will know if a cyberstalker is after them because all of their correspondence will be directed at them *personally*. This is not to be confused with the person who rants on his blog about the high price of oil or his frustration with the government over the lack of peace in the Middle East. Broad-based verbal attacks against large organizations are not considered to be harassment.

In addition to the personal vendetta many cyberstalkers have against their victims, they also have a tendency to disregard any sort of request, plea, or warning to cease their actions. Realize, however, that no matter how many times you've told a stalker "no," you *must* have written documentation to legally prove you have directly informed him to leave you or your children alone. Save your correspondence on your computer and print out a hard copy to keep as a backup file.

Finally, keep in mind that most of the online stalking cases that have been presented in court have involved one or more specific threats to inflict bodily harm directly to the target—in this case, your child. The threat must be credible, meaning it must be conceivable that the perpetrator could carry it out. Also, the threat must be made in such a way as to place a person in reasonable fear for his or her physical safety. Many kids who get involved with a cyberstalker don't see the stalking patterns materializing until *after* it's too late. For every child who takes the necessary precautions online and has full disclosure with his parents, there are countless others who have a complete lack of parental support. Their online "safety" strategy is little more than a game of chance and circumstance.[3]

GOOD NEWS

The news channels are filled with countless stories of young children being stalked and sometimes abducted by sexual predators online. Naturally, one of parents' first questions is, What would possess a child to engage in an intimate conversation with a total stranger? Yet maybe a better question to ask—and certainly one that hits closer to home—might be, What if *my son* is friends with one of these perpetrators? Or, Does my daughter have any online friends who might do something like this to *her?*

The good news is this: The number of reports of cyberstalking victims is relatively low when compared to the number of Internet users. There has been an increase in recent years in the number of reported sexual predators surfing the Internet looking for their next victims. And both parents and kids alike are making tremendous strides in practicing Internet safety. All of this is good news indeed!

Of course, this joy must be tempered with a sobering reality: As with all sexual assault cases, most experts agree that the relatively low number of reported events is actually due to the shame and humiliation victims often feel in reporting those crimes in the first place.

Don't let your child become a victim of a cyberstalker or sexual predator. As parents, you naturally do all you can to protect them when they're not at home. Show them the same care and concern when they're under your roof as well.

∽

Internet Protect Your Kids from Cyberstalkers and Sexual Predators by:

1. Teaching them that any solicitation from an unknown Internet or instant messaging source should be autom atically discarded.
2. Tracking the content and frequency of exchanges with suspected sexual predators or cyberstalkers.
3. Eliminating any pictures of your kids, postings of your home or cell phone number, or other sensitive information from social networking sites.
4. Reminding them that a person is not considered a stalker for responding to "flaming" your children may have initiated.
5. Knowing which cyberstalker laws apply in your state.

Chapter 4

WHEN INTERNET PORNOGRAPHY HITS HOME

Most eleven-year-old boys love to play video games. As far as Chris was concerned, there was nothing else he'd rather do. He was a decent student and enjoyed music, but it would be an understatement to say he was merely passionate about gaming.

His parents recognized that passion and encouraged him to pursue it, but in a balanced fashion. They enrolled him in a local workshop showing school-age kids how video games are created. They also gave him a subscription to a gaming magazine so he could read up on all the latest industry trends. And while he didn't play any games online, he still had his parents' approval to visit certain gaming Web sites that met with their prior approval.

Chris was pretty jazzed when he received an e-mail from his local video game store informing him that a sequel to one of his favorite games was about to be released. The e-mail included a link to a Web site where he could preview the game. But when he clicked on the link, he was surprised at what he saw. He had been redirected to a pornographic Web site and was now staring at the image of two naked women inviting him to take a free tour of their "XXX" site.

TRICKS OF THE TRADE

What happened to Chris is becoming a familiar experience for more and more kids his age: accidental exposure to Internet pornography. Fortunately for his parents, Chris was not actively pursuing porn online. Instead, he was the victim of what is known as a "doorway scam."

Here's how it works: A pornographer constructs a Web site that contains enough nonpornographic information that a search engine might consider it a match for a legitimate Web site—in this case, the site of a reputable video game manufacturer. In essence, it's a fake page set up to register enough attention that naive browsers will click through, only to be sent to the "real" page. The e-mail Chris received was legitimate, but when he clicked on the link, the "doorway scam" took affect and Chris was instead redirected to a porn site.[1]

The doorway scam is one of the most common tricks pornographers use to lure unsuspecting victims online. "Porn-napping" is another. It involves the purchase of a legitimate domain name whose owners have let the name lapse and have not renewed its registration. The internationally-known accounting firm of Ernst and Young fell victim to this scam once. Their children's money management site, www.moneyopolis.org, was porn-napped by pornographers who linked it to www.euro-teensluts.com. Anyone who typed in the Moneyopolis address got a rude surprise. The pornographers then required an exorbitant fee to release the domain name—sort of like a ransom demand.

"Cybersquatting" is a similar process whereby a pornographer will secure the rights to a domain name that is spelled similarly to a well-known site address. The most notorious example of this was when a pornographer secured the rights to the domain name www.whitehouse.com. Because the White House in Washington, D.C., is a part of the federal government, its e-mail address is actually www.whitehouse.gov. But suppose your ten-year-old daughter is doing a report on famous First Ladies and wants to find a comprehensive list of every President's wife who ever lived in the White House. Being the savvy Internet surfer she is, she forgoes the search engine and simply types "white-house.*com*" in the browser's address bar. The moment she hits "enter," she'll be redirected to a pornographic site instead—yet another victim of an online pornographer's trick.[2]

JUST THE FACTS

There are close to 400 million pages of online porn available for viewing on more than four million Web sites. Although this represents a little more than 10 percent of all the sites on the Internet worldwide, these sites are certainly generating considerable amounts of online traffic. There are nearly sixty-eight million pornographic search engine requests each day, which accounts for 25 percent of the daily total.[3]

With more kids spending time online, the chances for their risk of exposure to pornography dramatically increases. A whopping $1.5 billion will be spent on the purchase of pornographic CD-ROMs this year.[4] Another $2.5 billion will change hands in Internet-based pornographic transactions this year as well. And the child pornography industry will use a combination of books, magazines, photos, and online activity to generate yet another $3 billion in sales.

Overall, pornography in the United States is a $12 billion-a-year industry (worldwide, that number is a staggering $57 billion). To put that in perspective, consider the fact that the Big Three television networks—ABC, CBS, and NBC—have a combined total annual revenue of more than $6 billion dollars annually. According to the Internet Filter Review, the revenue generated by pornographic activity is even greater than the total revenue from all professional football, baseball, and basketball franchises in this country put together.[5]

The continued growth of the porn industry online is cause

for alarm, but what's even more concerning is *who* is driving it: kids. As stated in Chapter 1, the largest consumer group of Internet pornography is boys ages twelve to seventeen—which makes sense since the average age of a child's first Internet exposure to pornography is age eleven. A child who is exposed to what is known as a "soft-core" image in middle school soon runs the risk of seeking more "hard-core" fare. Oftentimes what fuels this desire is negative peer pressure.

PEER-TO-PEER NETWORKING

A majority of kids who get involved in using Internet porn don't set out to do so. They either receive it "accidentally" from an unknown source, or it is pushed to them by a friend online. The "pushing" process is also known as "peer-to-peer (P2P) networking," and it works like this: One friend in the cluster finds a pornographic image or video from a free site such as Limewire or Bearshare. He copies it to his computer and then "pushes" or forwards it to each member of his online mailing list. Many of these recipients then push it to *their* friends as well, and the viral marketing is on.

Now, not all of the P2P networking that takes place online is pornographic in nature. But the fact remains that 35 percent of all P2P downloads *are* related to porn. This represents an incredible 1.5 billion pornographic file downloads each month.[6] Could your kids be at risk of receiving one?

Sometimes a good kid like Chris winds up on the receiving end of a push like the one just described. The question then for parents is, How will you prepare your kids to deal with this kind of situation?

PORNOGRAPHIC CHRISTMAS CARDS . . . WHAT'S NEXT?

When my (Roger's) oldest daughter, Emmy, was in middle school, we gave her instant messaging privileges. She quickly created a profile and established a "buddy list" of kids who were known to our family. Emmy loved IMing with her friends while they did homework or played solitaire online. It was great fun for them.

One day around the start of Christmas break that year, she received an unsolicited e-mail from an individual whose screen name she didn't recognize. The subject line indicated this person was looking for other "soccer friends" to "hook up with." Though she wasn't familiar with the e-mail address, Emmy opened it anyway. What she found was a picture of a woman standing next to a Christmas tree and wearing nothing but an elf's hat and a smile.

Emmy quickly told her mom and then showed her the e-mail and attached photo. My wife immediately took action and responded to the e-mail, notifying both the sender and our Internet service provider at the time (America Online) that this photo had been sent to a twelve-year-old girl. Amazingly, the woman who originally sent the picture responded by saying she was sorry if we were offended but that she didn't see anything wrong with "looking for other soccer lovers who wanted to have a little fun."

Our natural tendency as parents is to assume that something like this will never happen to our kids. But the reality is, it *can* . . . and it *does*. Recent statistics indicate that as much as *90 percent* of kids ages eight to sixteen have viewed pornography online during the last year—and most of the time while they were doing homework.[7] This doesn't necessarily mean that kids are browsing for porn while they're trying to figure out geometry. But sometimes the pornographic images somehow "find" your kids. And believe me, it's quite a shock when they do!

Looking back on the Christmas card incident today, I realize that we weren't really prepared to handle that kind of situation. My wife *did* contact our Internet service provider (ISP) immediately, but we had never even heard of Web filters or spam blockers at that time. Technology has changed quite a bit since then, and there are now plenty of protective software programs available that can easily be installed at home to *Internet Protect*

Your Kids against the dangers of unsolicited Internet pornography. In addition, consider the following measures:

1. Talk to your kids about what could happen.

Have your response plan in place *before* you face a situation like ours, if at all possible. If one of your kids has already been victimized once before, work through your response plan before it happens again. Talk to your children about what to do if they receive a pornographic e-mail—how they should tell you immediately but not delete the e-mail right away. You'll need to respond to both the sender as well as your ISP so they can take action. You'll also want to keep a copy as well to have on hand as documented proof of the assault.

2. Install a spam blocker.

Utilizing a "spam blocker" (a deterrent for online junk mail) can prevent your kids from receiving unwanted e-mail. This kind of tool features a mechanism that is set to identify a key word in either the sender's e-mail address or in the subject line of the correspondence. If the scanner senses the e-mail is spam, it won't let it through.

The Web filter you install on your family's computer should give you a variety of different options in terms of the categories or keywords you choose to block. A quality filtering system should enable you to block access to and monitor certain chat rooms. You should also be able to filter or completely block selected e-mail and pop-ups as well. (For a complete list of recommended filters, see Appendix F.)

3. Report suspicious behavior.

Make it a habit to report any suspicious e-mail you or your child receives to your ISP. It doesn't have to be hard-core pornography to be offensive. Sometimes kids are on the receiving end of e-mail that is sexually suggestive but includes no photo attachments. It's still considered sexual harassment and should be investigated. If it looks like pornography to you, your ISP needs to know about it!

NOT JUST A MAN'S WORLD

If it appears that the porn industry caters more to men, that's because more males use pornography than females. The most recent research indicates that of all the visitors to pornographic Web sites, 72 percent are men and 28 percent women. However, studies show that the women and girls who *do* use pornography are more likely to use it more often than men. In fact, females are twice as likely to utilize a pornographic chat room as males.[8]

How are women and young girls lured into a predominantly male-oriented underworld? Often it's through the casual merging of teen sites with overt pornographers, as has been the case with MySpace and Playboy. When MySpace began its meteoric expansion during late 2005 and early 2006, executives at Playboy took notice. Determined to capitalize on the site's increasing popularity, the magazine created a contest to find "The Girls of MySpace." More than 150 girls responded. Eventually the field was narrowed down to the nine finalists, who were then featured in a layout for the print edition of the magazine.

Web Filters and MySpace

You may think the chances of your children accidentally stumbling onto a profile promoting a Playboy magazine centerfold may be small. But given the 100 million-plus profiles from which to choose, there's a good possibility they might find something on MySpace you don't want them to see.

If you're going to allow your children to have MySpace profiles, make sure you sit down with them to insure it's established to be as safe as possible. Install a good Web filter and make sure they practice the basics of Internet safety. However, if you're not convinced that they are ready to handle a potential hazard as a result of going on MySpace, prohibit its use in your home.

By tapping into the MySpace community, Playboy obviously hoped to increase magazine sales. But in addition to the spike in newsstand revenue, the company also received something far more valuable: immeasurable free publicity via the individual MySpace profiles of each girl who submitted photos for the contest.

From a marketing standpoint, the move was brilliant, especially when you consider the viral nature of a social networking site. Take the 150 profiles who entered, figure that each has an average of at least 150 online friends, then do the math. Tens of thousands of profiles could have been hit with "bulletins" (online announcements) from each of the contestants publicizing that they were trying to "friend" as many people as possible so the execs at Playboy would consider them worthy for placement in the Girls of MySpace layout.

BROWSING WITH EASE

Before we continue, it is worth noting that while doing research for another segment of this book, our research team was introduced to this contest through a simple browse of existing MySpace profiles. The "browse" function on MySpace enables users to view the profiles of other users. Since there are more than 100 million profiles available, browsing works in much the same way the "shuffle" operates on an MP3 player. Every time the browse button is clicked, a different collection of profiles is presented on the screen based on the parameters you establish—the age range you'd like to explore; whether you're looking to meet men, women, or both; and the geographic location of the profile holder. Each time our team browsed, we set the parameters as "18-100" for age, "both" for gender, and "any" for location.

During one browsing session in particular, we clicked on the picture of a girl who turned out to be one of the finalists in "The Girls of MySpace" contest. A Google search ensued, and we had the particulars about the contest and the actual issue of the magazine within a matter of minutes.

Of the nine finalists who were featured in the layout, six of them had MySpace profiles boasting more than 1,000 "friends." In fact, the two most popular girls counted more than 44,000 friends on each of their profiles, including several participants in the porn industry. For the record, that same session also uncovered two other "aspiring models" on MySpace, one of whom had more than 100,000 friends, and the other 225,534 at last count.

Our research team discovered this porn connection by establishing a MySpace profile, engaging the browse function, and then clicking on a profile at random based solely on one picture—something your teenage son or daughter could have also done just as easily. As stated earlier, the management of MySpace works as diligently as they can to remove pornographic images and other content they deem harmful and unworthy for their Web site. But with more than 100 million profiles to monitor, the odds are high that they will not be able to delete everything that needs removing. Our brief and unsophisticated research proved that within minutes.

CONFESSIONS OF AN ONLINE "CAMKID"

Children are attracted to the Internet for a number of reasons. And, as long as there are kids online, there will be any number of deviants looking to prey upon them. Not every kid will be victimized, but sometimes one child's pain will motivate thousands of parents to do all we can to *Internet Protect Our Kids*.

Justin Berry's story has done just that.

He is rail-thin with a smile that sometimes looks more like a scowl. He appears cool in a "computer geek" sort of way and has a mysterious, deep-set stare that would cause any teenage girl to blush if she thought it was meant just for her. Justin has a vulnerability about him that could make half of his teachers nominate him for student of the year . . . and the other half wonder if they can actually trust him or not.

But no one would ever suspect that Justin used to be a "camkid"—a Webcam pornographer—whose innocent venture in online social networking led him right to the center of a criminal operation the likes our society had never seen before.

Just seven years ago, Justin's life was not much different from many other thirteen-year olds he knew. Justin was a nerd of sorts who liked spending his free hours online. He even started a legitimate small business in his spare time helping other kids establish their own Web sites. Justin began hanging out online for typical teenage-boy reasons: He wanted to make some new friends and possibly meet a few girls who had the same interests he did—music and computers, among others.

Dial-up vs. High-Speed Internet Connection
Almost three-fourths of all homes with Internet connections in the United States now access the Web using a high-speed connection such as broadband or DSL.[9] The advantages of having a faster connection are fairly obvious: less time spent waiting to connect and typically less time spent perusing your favorite Web sites.

One downside of a high-speed connection, however, is the fact that it seldom, if ever, disconnects. This is one area where dial-up service is preferable. While considerably slower than broadband, the dial-up option does give you more flexibility in terms of disconnecting your service altogether. This makes it easier to escape a connection to a pornographic Web site, accidental or otherwise.

Like most kids who go online looking for friendship, Justin figured that all of his new acquaintances were other kids. So when one of his "friends" told him that he'd give Justin $50 for taking off his shirt while they were chatting online, Justin agreed. He hooked up a simple Webcam to his computer, then logged onto an online payment site. Once the transaction was complete, Justin took off his shirt and continued chatting . . . entering the dark underworld of Internet porn without even realizing he was doing anything wrong.

A BOY BECOMES A PORNOGRAPHER

Within days, more of Justin's new online friends began e-mailing him with requests of their own, such as, "Would you chat with me online wearing only your boxers?" The more risqué the request, the more money Justin was offered. The requests grew more sexually suggestive until, eventually, he was masturbating regularly in view of his Webcam for a growing number of paying friends.

Even as his customers' demands became more lurid and obscene, Justin continued to comply because he reasoned this was just normal behavior for a thirteen-year-old—only he was getting paid for it. Not only did the money continue to roll in, but his new and growing list of friends showed him how he could also establish an online "wish list." Justin could register for the latest in computer gear and his friends would give it to him, as long as he continued to perform.

At this point, you may be wondering how Justin hid his secret life from his parents for so long. In fact, his mother, Karen, *did* know that her son had established a legitimate Internet business; she just didn't know it wasn't the same one he'd started with. Whenever Justin received a shipment from a friend, she naturally assumed it was from one of his actual clients. But, over time, even Karen noticed a change in her son's behavior.

Though she was concerned about the dramatic increase in time Justin spent alone in his bedroom, his mother chalked it up to general teen moodiness. She had installed protective software on his computer, so she never suspected his Internet activity would be at the heart of the problem. Karen just figured his mood swings and sullen attitude were the result of the general aches and pains of making the transition from middle school to high school.

Justin's stepfather, meanwhile, left the situation for his wife to handle, because if anyone could spot a child in serious trouble, it was Karen. Her work with sexually abused children made her uniquely qualified to work with such a situation—or so she thought.

A STAR AT SIXTEEN

By the time he turned sixteen, Justin had become an online porn star among Internet pedophiles. One customer offered Justin a large sum of money—thousands of dollars over time—to meet him in Las Vegas for the weekend. Justin agreed to go, told his mother he was heading to a computer convention with a friend, and then made the trip. Once he arrived, he was sexually molested repeatedly. But the abuse didn't stop there; upon his return home, Justin discovered that this man had rented an apartment close to Justin's mother's house so that Justin could spend more time "entertaining" him on his Webcam without Karen growing too suspicious.

As time went by and the money continued to pour in, Justin sank deeper into depression. When news of his online activities was leaked to a classmate, Justin was fearful his mother would find out about his secret life, so he asked to be allowed to visit his biological father, who was living in Mexico at the time. It was then and there that Justin told his dad the truth about his Webcam business, explaining he had made so much money over the past four years he was able to finance his own trip south of the border.

Though Justin's revelation was an eye-opener, his father did not give him the counsel he was hoping for. Not only did his dad not stop him from his pornographic endeavors, he actually showed him how to *maximize his earning potential*. Incredibly, the man Justin trusted with a secret so dark that no child should ever have to endure it was willing to continue the exploitation of his son in the name of increased profits.

Justin continued his lifestyle of pornography, filming himself having intercourse with prostitutes, and then broadcasting their sexual escapades online. Justin's dad contributed to the financial success of the business by finding willing prostitutes for his son to have sex with online. The Web site was more lucrative than ever, but Justin's depression over his lifestyle led him to delve deeper into drug and alcohol abuse.

AN UNLIKELY FRIENDSHIP

At the same time Justin's life was spinning out of control, an investigative reporter from *The New York Times* was researching a story on Internet fraud. His exploration led him to a Web site where an online dialog was taking place. The topic was child pornography, and the center of discussion was a young boy named Justin.

The reporter could tell right away from the tone of the online conversation that this boy needed help. So, through perseverance and providence, he was able to connect with Justin online. It took several months of dialoging before the reporter would earn the boy's trust, but eventually he did.

By the time the reporter met Justin in person, the "camkid" who had become a larger-than-life porn king was an emaciated drug addict. Fortunately, over time Justin began to open up to his new friend. He regained his physical strength and stopped using drugs. Still, he had an even bigger challenge ahead of him. Justin had enough information at his disposal to bring countless pornographers, credit card companies, and other adult enterprises to justice. These associates were the ones who helped him build an online business that was paying the teenager thousands of dollars a week, and obviously, they wouldn't take kindly to having this kid turn on them. And what about Justin's online friends? He could help press charges against these pedophiles as well—if they didn't kill him first.

Eventually Justin took the bravest step of his young life and agreed to cooperate with authorities to press charges against his former clients and associates. He shut down his Web site and spent the next six months walking the reporter through the Webcam pornography business. Despite the tremendous guilt and shame Justin felt in running this operation, he nonetheless was diligent in keeping detailed records of his online chats and business transactions—records that would help law enforcement prosecute the men who had sexually exploited him.

The list included counselors, school teachers, pediatricians, even an attorney who represented children in abuse and custody cases. In other words, the very individuals to whom we look to *enhance* the quality of our children's lives, not to rob them of their childhood and future dignity.

Many of those same men were able to figure out that it was Justin who blew the whistle on their criminal activity. Since shutting down his Webcam operation and cooperating with the FBI, Justin has received countless death threats and currently lives in seclusion.[10]

Learning from Justin's Story

Obviously, Justin's story is extreme. Yet just one case like his is one too many. What started out with a love of computers, a desire to make new friends, a Webcam and $50, turned into an odyssey of sexual and drug abuse, and the scarring of a young boy's soul.

No family should ever have to experience such a violation because of a breakdown in communication. And no child should ever have to pay such a high price just to experience the kind of connection we all crave. Justin's mother thought she had taken all the necessary precautions to keep her son safe online. She

---

Delete a Profile If Necessary

As a parent, part of the Internet Usage Agreement you draft with your children should include a provision for you or your spouse to remove from their social networking profile any item you deem offensive. You may be facing a situation right now where your child's MySpace profile is offensive, distasteful, or simply inappropriate beyond repair. That being the case, we highly recommend deleting it altogether. Only after a discussion about the kind of content you can both agree is appropriate should MySpace privileges be reinstated. (For more information on how to delete a MySpace profile, see Appendix C.)

---

thought she knew Justin well enough to trust him when he said everything in his life was "all right."

She was wrong. And none of us as parents can ever afford to be that misinformed. Now more than ever, we need to *Internet Protect Our Kids* from the dangers of pornography.

Internet Protect Your Kids from Online Pornography by:

1. Utilizing a spam blocker to prevent them from receiving unwanted e-mail.
2. Preparing them for what to do when a pornographic e-mail or an e-mail with a link to a pornographic site makes its way through your filter.
3. Reporting any suspicious e-mail you or your child receives to your Internet service provider. If it looks like pornography to you, your ISP needs to know about it!
4. Installing a Web filtering system to keep them from accessing pornographic sites.
5. Considering using a dial-up ISP rather than maintaining an uninterruptible connection through a broadband, high-speed connection.

Chapter 5

A Multimedia Community

"Music, TV, movies, friends—these are what attracted people to MySpace. There has never been a social network you could buy your way into [until MySpace came along]."
—MySpace co-founder, Chris DeWolfe[1]

I've heard so many stories about MySpace, I don't know *what* to think."

Kristin is a single mother of three. She has a fifteen-year-old son and two daughters, ages fourteen and eleven. All three of her kids have been hounding her to let them set up MySpace profiles. She's not so sure that's a good idea.

"So many of their friends have MySpace pages," Kristin says. "Okay, it seems like *all* of their friends do. But every time I see one of those reports on TV about some teenage girl running away from home to meet up with her MySpace boyfriend in a different state, I wonder if *my* kids might get tricked into doing something like that, too."

What mother *doesn't* worry about the safety of her children?

Keep Your Plans to Yourself

At HomeWord one of the key principles that guides our ministry is found in Proverbs 22:6: "Train up a child in the way he should go, and when he is old he will not depart from it" (NKJV). Teaching our children to stay safe online has never been more crucial than it is right now. One of the easiest and most immediate ways you can do that is to let your kids know the importance of never using the Internet to tell their friends what their plans are for the day. Oftentimes kids will leave their whereabouts on their "away message" (these are messages that are automatically sent to others when a user isn't active on IM—similar to a voice message on an answering machine). For example, a common IM or chat-room away is, "Going to the park with my best friend," or "Parents gone. Takin' a shower. Call my cell if you want to connect—949.555.3134." Messages like these give sexual predators all the information they need to either reach your kids by phone or track down their profiles online—which, as we've already discussed, can be the first step to grooming them as the next sexual victim.

And yet, not *every* kid who goes online winds up dropping out of school and moving to the Middle East with their "online love."

"I like using the Internet," Kristin acknowledges, "and I trust that my kids will use it responsibly. And this whole MySpace thing really fascinates me. But what do I do? Do I let my children use it? I mean, why are so many kids addicted to MySpace?"

In Chapter 2 we briefly covered some of the reasons teens and preteens are flocking to social networking sites such as MySpace by the millions. We highlighted the personal expression aspect that draws so many users. Adolescents, who are already in an age where defining who they are is a crucial step of self-identification, have the opportunity to establish their own unique identity without the risk of being singled out too much. We also briefly touched on the sense of belonging these online networking sites bring.

In this chapter, we'll expand on this and explain just why kids today have made MySpace, the Internet at large, and several other media forms such an integral part of their lives. While the driving force behind this is a universal need, Generation @ seems to be especially overt in its desire for one thing: *community*.

VIRTUALLY MOLDED TOGETHER

The under-twenty-five crowd is made up of the original "Gymboree Kids." Many of them spent more time during their early years in playgroups and cultivating "friendship clusters" than they did with their own families. As a result, they are driven by a high sense of community that doesn't require family participation. To most of us, that would mean more time spent hanging out with friends in coffee shops, malls, movie theaters, and clubs. We expect these youngsters to be an extension of a *Friends* episode, with groups hanging out at all hours of the day at a central location while members come and go.

Yet only a few years after the final *Friends* episode, that concept and those surroundings have already, for the most part, become extinct. And a major reason for that is this generation's strong connection to technology and media. We must remember the fact that *computers have always been a part of their lives*. Most have no idea what life was like pre-Internet. And it's evident in their use.

Consider the following statistics unveiled by the Pew Internet and American Life Project:

- 87 percent of all teenagers in America use the Internet.
- 60 percent of all sixth-graders use the Internet. By the time kids reach the eleventh grade, that number jumps to a whopping *94 percent*. (The middle-school years are when a teen is most likely to start going online on a regular basis.)
- 83 percent of teenagers surveyed reported that "most" of the people they know use the Internet.
- 84 percent of teenagers own at least one of the following: computer, cell phone, or PDA.

- 81 percent of teens say they use the Internet to play games online.
- 89 percent of all teens use e-mail; 75 percent also use instant messaging.
- 82 percent of teens who IM use a message blocker to keep away unwanted messages.
- 32 percent of teens IM every day.[2]

Guard Personal Information

Teach your children to never give out any personal information online (name, age, home address, home or cell phone number, parent's name, etc.). If your kids do earn social networking privileges, make sure they know to never fill out any form or online questionnaire that would ask such sensitive information. Social networking sites are notorious for circulating "things you need to know about me" surveys. They look harmless, and kids love filling them out and then pushing them to all their online friends. Don't let them fall into the trap of offering potentially damaging information about themselves this way.

The Internet is more than just a modern convenience for teens and preteens. It's become an integral part of everyday life, and *kids* have been the driving force behind its increasing popularity. At present, almost 30 percent of kids between the ages of eight and fifteen say the Internet is their primary source of communication. What's more, 54 percent of those kids feel that by 2010 they'll be spending more time online than they will playing organized sports.[3] More and more kids are choosing to use the Internet as the hub of all their communication. Factor in these two elements—technology and the need for community—and you can see why a concept like MySpace would have universal appeal to Generation @.

I WANT MY MTV!

It's no secret that kids and young adults experience a sense of community when they go online. All of their friends are there networking, so it seems like both a safe place and a part of who they are.

The question is, *How did they get here?* When did entertainment become such a dominant force in the lives of young people that parents would have to work so hard to have influence in their lives? To answer that question, we have to look back to the last time America's youth was so transfixed by the confluence of multiple media and entertainment influences.

On August 1, 1981, an upstart cable television channel called MTV was broadcast on TV sets across the United States for the first time. Music videos were a relatively obscure form of promoting popular music at the time, but industry executives praised the leadership at MTV for its creative vision. Back then it seemed hard to imagine that teens and children would willingly sit around watching videos of their favorite musicians lip-syncing to their big hits, but it turns out that they would. Before long, adolescents were watching MTV an average of ten hours a week—just under an hour and a half every day. Yet the strategists who launched this media phenomenon weren't surprised at the response.

"Early on, we made a key decision that (MTV) would be the voice of young America," former MTV president and CEO Robert Pittman said. "We were building more than just a channel; we were building a culture."[4]

Indeed they were. As the music network's popularity grew, it seemed like every kid in America was shouting, "I want my MTV!" And they got it. By the end of 1981, MTV was available in more than two million U.S. homes. And its influence has continued to this day. Though it is still ostensibly a "music television" channel, MTV has morphed into the standard-bearer for reality TV programming, single and album promotion, fashion styles, catch phrases, and overall pop-culture trendsetting. On its twenty-fifth anniversary in 2006, MTV was viewed in more than 440 million homes in 168 countries worldwide.[5]

The lure of MTV led to teens to spending countless hours each week glued to the tube. But times have changed, and over the past few years, kids began making the shift to the Internet. With teens mixing up their entertainment choices—a little MySpace here, a little iPod there—rather than sitting exclusively in front of their television sets, MTV took notice (as always) and now offers a multiplatform barrage of content available in every format. Why the quick shift? The average teen now spends as many as twenty-six hours a month online,[6] and more than one-third are on the Web for three or more hours a day.[7]

FROM MEDIA TO MEDIA

This current transition from TV to the Internet (or at least a blend of the two) really shouldn't be a surprise to us as parents, because the fact is that we like to use the Internet, too. We're way too cool to be bound to "old-fashioned" sources for information like newspapers or phone books. Most of us have already discovered that it's much easier and faster to simply find the resources we're looking for via a search engine from Yahoo or Google.

Is it any wonder, then, that we "cool parents" are raising such "ultracool" kids who have now taken Internet use to the proverbial next level? Kids are the driving force in the popularity of social networking sites such as Xanga, Facebook, and the behemoth that has changed the face of online communication, MySpace. But Internet use goes well beyond social networking. So-called "e-commerce" is growing in a number of other product categories as well, and it affects more than just your PC or Mac. Consider the evolution of the cell phone.

If you owned a portable phone in the mid-1990s, you accessed analog phone lines from a handheld device that was basically the length and width of a mid-size walkie-talkie. Though bulky, the first mobile phones gave individuals more flexibility in the ways they could communicate. Still, this was "horse and buggy" technology in comparison to modern-day portable communication.

The standard handheld device today offers call waiting, voice-mail, text-messaging, and IMing services. Some serve as PDAs by which users can keep track of appointments, important phone numbers and addresses, and other useful personal data.

Chatting with Strangers

Lindsay was about to make a potentially life-changing decision based on emotions that exceeded her maturity level. Her infatuation began when she responded to an invitation to go into a chat room with a guy she had never actually met in person before.

It's crucial that we teach our kids to never respond to an unsolicited invitation to "chat." Requests like these for contact should always be rejected. You know who your friends are, and new ones don't just come from out of nowhere on the Internet!

Wireless Internet access is growing in availability for the portable phone. Couple that with the advancement of MP3, video, and streaming technology, and the average cell phone is rapidly becoming a mobile media and entertainment center.

The hand-in-glove relationship between the cell phone and the Internet is easy for most parents to miss at first glance. Perhaps that's because, of the 66 percent of adults who own at least one cell phone, only 14 percent use it to connect to the Internet. Teens and young adults are a different story. Though fewer Generation @ members own cell phones (45 percent of teens, with that figure inching upward each day),[8] a larger percentage (28) of them go online via their cell phone.[9] They play online games, surf the Web for on-the-spot information, download songs or videos, or check their favorite sites.

TEXT-MESSAGING INTO TROUBLE

Obviously, to use all these features costs money. The most basic cell-phone coverage plans today involve strictly the monthly service charges for the actual use of the phone. Text messaging obviously adds to those fees, though many providers offer bulk rates for unlimited texting to help manage those costs.

Yet sometimes keeping tabs on the financial aspect of using a cell phone doesn't take into consideration the emotional investment. Natalie discovered this in shocking fashion. Her fourteen-year-old daughter, Lindsay, had met a guy on an SNS. They had gotten to know each other better in an online chat room, then decided to take their conversations off-line. So they communicated through text messaging.

Lindsay *thought* her new boyfriend was a nineteen-year-old college sophomore, but he turned out to be twenty-five. She, too, had misrepresented herself online, indicating that she was a

---

No Online Purchases by Kids

Parents usually view the cell phone as a means of making it easier to keep their families connected when life gets too crazy. Kids, meanwhile, are more likely to see their cell as a fashion accessory than a safety tool. But the reality is that cell phone safety is a key step to Internet protecting your kids. The gadgetry kids like to download from the Internet to their cell phones is usually fairly inexpensive. Although the costs seem low to them, the actual price they may wind up paying in terms of loss of privacy could turn out to be far greater than they can afford.

Instruct your children to never enter an area of the Internet that requires some form of guarantee for payment such as a credit card. Such sites will explain that the card imprint is only for "security" purposes or to verify that the person about to enter that site is at least eighteen years of age. But most kids can figure out how to use a credit card to access any site they'd like. And the reality is, once a site operator has your credit card info, you've left yourself wide open for fraudulent activity to be conducted at your expense—literally!

---

freshman in college and, thus, also nineteen.

Because of the flat fee their cell plan provided each month for unlimited text-messaging, Natalie paid little attention to the actual number of text messages Lindsay was sending and receiving each month. But one day, she got curious and actually read through the details of her cell phone bill. It revealed no fewer than 17,000 text messages between her fourteen-year-old daughter and the twenty-five-year-old suitor that month . . . and 19,000 the month before.

When Natalie pressed her daughter to see what all these messages could possibly be about, Lindsay was hesitant at first, but she reluctantly agreed to show her mother a few samples. The text message-based relationship started out innocently enough but was escalating into something much deeper. Lindsay's new boyfriend was pressuring her to go away for the weekend together with him, and she had actually been in the process of making plans to do so just as her mother intervened.

ACCESSORIZE TO CUSTOMIZE

The next potential trouble spots for parents in dealing with the cell phone/Internet connection deal with two of the major profit centers for cell phone usage: video gaming and ringtones. Because many phones come preloaded with popular mobile games, it's not unusual to see a kid actually use his phone as a gaming device more than a vehicle for communication. The preloaded games simply whet the appetite; they're a successful lure to get a kid interested in downloading other, newer games that usually involve fees.

If you give your kids unlimited access to downloading games from the Internet to their cell phones, you may be unknowingly encouraging your kids to seek out more potentially dangerous online sites in the process.

Ringtones, meanwhile, are yet another means for users to

customize their cell phone. The ringtone revolution hit the recorded music industry like wildfire, and the blaze hasn't stopped burning yet. The process is actually simple: An artist will make a short portion of one of her popular songs available for downloading at a minimal cost, usually under $1 per song. The user then downloads the snippet into his phone, replacing the standard ringtone options originally available on the unit.

The practice has become so widespread that the Recording Industry Association of America (RIAA) now recognizes ringtone downloads in the same way it acknowledges sales of audio CDs and DVDs. Ringtone downloading has emerged as a multi-*billion*-dollar business, yet it's also a deceptively "harmless" entryway for teens and preteens into extensive Internet use that plagues so many of their peers.

DIGITAL MUSIC AND PROGRAMS ON THE GO

Music has always played a vital role in the lives of teens and pre-teens, so it makes sense that the advent of MP3 technology has led to a shift in the way recorded music is distributed and purchased. The trip to the local record store to buy a couple of CDs is being replaced by the process of downloading songs through sites such as iTunes onto a computer or portable MP3 player.

The growth in popularity of the iPod and other portable recorder/players has also given birth to a new form of broadcasting known as "podcasting." This is a means of distributing electronic multimedia files to portable devices via the Internet using several Web sites that serve as "syndication feeds" (centers that continuously collect and distribute files). Literally tens of thousands of video and audio programs primarily produced for commercial television and radio are made available for downloading—typically without cost—onto mobile devices such as cell phones, iPods, or MP3 players.

Recently, television networks have been scrambling to podcast their shows for those wanting to watch "on the go." Churches and other nonprofit organizations have also gotten into the podcasting act, making sermons, Bible studies, and even entire worship services available in podcast form. The same holds true for general businesses, with industry giants such as General Motors and IBM creating market-segment advertising campaigns driven exclusively by podcasts and created specifically for those target audiences.

(While we're on the subject of podcasting, two podcasts we highly recommend are *New Life Live!* and *HomeWord with Jim Burns.* For more information on how you can download these programs, go to www.newlife.com and www.homeword.com.)

THE INTERNET AND YOUR CHILD'S SCHOOL

Though much of what's profitable online is entertainment-oriented, the educational arena is also being shaped by the growth and influence of the Internet. Students as young as eleven and twelve are being directed to school district-sponsored Web sites that allow them to check up on grades or receive homework assignments. Parents can also use these sites as well, and they're usually encouraged to do so to keep up on their children's projects. Want to avoid those assignments that seem to come up at the last minute but were actually part of the course outline the entire semester? Try looking online!

Suffice it to say that the influence of Internet on those under the age of twenty-five has led to the creation of a worldwide virtual community. While this online "family" can sometimes pacify a universal need among this generation, it frequently leads teens and preteens into a false intimacy online that can often prove harmful. How we as parents learn to deal with this new reality could possibly be the difference between life and death for our kids . . . so it's up to us to be proactive in getting informed.

ॐ

**Internet Protect Your Kids from
Dangerous Online "Friendships" by:**

1. Deleting their MySpace profile if necessary. (See Appendix C for details.)
2. Keeping their chat-room and IM away messages completely generic.
3. Teaching them to keep personal information off the Internet.
4. Instructing them to never enter an area of the Internet that requires a credit card for entry, even if the site claims to be free.
5. Affirming them when they reject an unsolicited request to enter into a chat room.

Chapter 6

HELPING YOUR CHILD DEAL WITH AN ONLINE BULLY

Julia was the kind of girl everyone in school wanted to get to know. She was both a cheerleader and an athlete, so there weren't too many kids in her mid-size high school who didn't know who she was.

Matt had been trying to get Julia's attention since the third grade, but with no luck. So when a buddy offered to give him the girl's IM screen name, he jumped at the chance. He started sending her messages, but she didn't respond. In all honesty, she didn't really recognize his screen name, and she wasn't the type who would talk to just anybody online. This frustrated Matt, so he decided to take some rather desperate measures to get Julia to notice him: He threatened to kill her if she wouldn't go out with him.

Obviously, Julia was a little freaked out by Matt's message at first. After she gathered her composure, she got up the nerve to tell her mom about the threat. Julia's mother wasted no time; she called the local police department, and they started an investigation.

You may have never received a death threat via e-mail before. But there's a good chance you *have* been on the receiving end of a rather sternly worded correspondence from a person who turned out to be far less vicious in person than he was online. A message can easily get mangled and intentions misunderstood when there isn't face-to-face communication. With kids, this kind of situation only gets worse.

MEAN GIRLS

It's no secret that kids can be pretty cruel to each other at times. But the increase in the number of girls bullying other girls on high school and middle school campuses is of particular cause for alarm.

On a recent edition of the HomeWord radio program, we talked with youth-culture observer Hayley DiMarco. She's now a happily married mother and author, but during her teenage years, she was the victim of the relentless bullying of a couple of girls at the small Christian school she attended. Her bullies actually developed a scoring system whereby each would earn a point for committing a hateful act against her victim—in this case, young Hayley. They also scored if they were able to get her to retaliate against them.[1]

The Internet was not a factor for the bullies who hassled Hayley DiMarco, but it does play a role in the way bullies harass their victims today. Ryan Halligan's parents know just how dangerous online bullying can be.

AN EASY MARK

By the time he reached middle school, Ryan thought he had faced his fears and defeated them. Ever since a bully started picking on him with a couple of buddies in the fifth grade, Ryan had lived on an emotional roller coaster. Now it appeared that things were finally beginning to even out—or at least that's what his parents thought.

School was always something of a challenge for Ryan. He wasn't exactly the smartest or most athletic kid in his class. He always gave his best effort, but preadolescent children aren't big on awarding "A's for effort" in the classroom or on the play-ground. A couple of aspiring young goons made Ryan for an easy mark, and the bullying was on.

Over the next two years, their taunting and teasing was relentless. So, in an effort to help his son develop better physical coordination and a healthier self-image, Ryan's dad enrolled both he and his son in a kickboxing program. It seemed to work. Ryan loved working out with his dad, and his physical coordina-

---

Do Not Retaliate

If your child has been victimized by a bully online, she may want to retaliate. Don't go there. A kid who tries to bully another child online is in no frame of mind to negotiate. The best solution is to not engage or interact with the cyberbully at all. Save your energy for more important actions, like keeping a log of any and every incident of online abuse that your child encounters. Save any e-mail or IM communication your child has with the bully. You may want to create a separate folder in your computer for storing these correspondences. Also, be sure to print out a hard copy of the day's exchanges as well. Should the bullying lead to a criminal action, your records will prove most helpful to the law enforcement officials assigned to your child's case.

---

tion steadily improved. John Halligan stressed with his son that he should never use these techniques to *start* an altercation, but *finishing* one was a completely different story!

It shouldn't have come as a surprise, then, when John received a call from Ryan's school one day that his son had been involved in a fight. The bully had started it, but Ryan hung in there right with him. Afterward, he seemed to have gained a new measure of self-respect, which made his parents proud.

That pride soon turned to concern when Ryan announced shortly after the fight that his former nemesis was now his "good friend." Against their better judgment, the Halligans chose not to intervene—a decision they would soon come to regret.

Don't Get Burned by Flaming

Teach your kids to recognize flame mail when they see it. "Flaming" is Internet slang for when someone sends a message to purposefully incite the recipient. Some bullies will try to bait their victims into trying to defend themselves against false accusations. Let your kids know that they don't need to take the bait. Simply save the "flame" and file it. It may come in handy later on.

BURNED BY FLAME MAIL

Ryan had been active online for a couple of years at that point, and he seemed to relish his Internet communication with the former bully and other friends, including a cute girl from his middle school he had a crush on. But Ryan's attitude became more sullen again over time, even more withdrawn than he'd ever been during the worst of the bullying he'd received in elementary school. Still, his parents kept their distance, hoping their son would be able to work through his issues on his own.

The middle schooler did all he could to convince his parents that nothing was wrong, that his former tormentor was now his friend. But in reality, that simply wasn't true. Turns out that the bullying did *not* end after the fight that day; it merely shifted to the Internet and grew even more intense. The bully who befriended Ryan convinced the shy boy to share some of his deepest personal secrets—and then spread them around by posting them on his online profile.

Sometimes the bully would utilize "flame mail" (an e-mail blast designed to agitate or embarrass the recipient). "Flaming" typically involves copying the flame mail to as many people as possible—in this case, several hundred kids from Ryan's middle school. The pain and humiliation of this constant online tormenting proved to be too much for Ryan. He eventually found solace with a couple of other new friends online, boys who were convinced that the only way to escape the pain of their lives was to end them once and for all.

Ryan Halligan was just thirteen years old when he took his own life. It was only after his death that his father began to understand the depth of the terror Ryan lived through every day online. He started reading through his son's IMs and discovered how cruel kids can be to each other. At the height of the harassment, even kids who didn't even know Ryan were getting in on the bullying as well.[2]

IS YOUR CHILD BEING BULLIED ONLINE?

At this point, you may be asking yourself, Is one of *my* children the victim of a cyberbully right now? That's a fair question, especially if you've never had this kind of conversation with your kids before. Based on the latest research, you might want to have that discussion sooner than later.

In 2001, around 6 percent of all kids who went online reported harassment from a cyberbully. By 2006, that figure had risen to 9 percent.[3] And as more kids spend a greater amount of time online and less time engaged in meaningful activities and relationships, there's a good chance that number will grow to double digits in the next couple of years, if not sooner.

Bullying has always been a part of adolescence, and the cyberbully does bear a resemblance to the thug in school who went around giving wedgies and stuffing kids in trashcans.

When we were growing up, most of the boys could quickly figure out who the "tough guys" were. We had to decide either to stand and fight them or find creative ways to avoid them. The same held true on the other side of the playground, as the "mean girls" would rule their part of the school with cunning, conniving, and catty behavior.

Bullies didn't limit their tormenting ways to just the schoolyard. They also took their terrorizing ways into neighborhoods, parks, shopping malls, and video arcades—anywhere kids used to hang out. Today, the cyberbully strikes in many of the same ways that the traditional school thug used to, with one major difference: The cyberbully can attack you even when you're not around. In fact, you may not even know whether or not you're being attacked. All it takes is one text message insinuating an embarrassing revelation about someone (for example, "Dude, Jeff told me he's *gay!*"), and that message will be posted and pushed to literally thousands of Internet and cell phone users in a matter of seconds.

ANONYMOUS BULLYING

"I got some anonymous e-mails—probably around 300 of them—and they all had the same message on them, saying that I was a whore."

That's the confession of a fifteen-year-old girl who unknowingly became a victim of cyberbullying. She honestly had no idea who would start such a rumor, but she suspected it might have

---

Identifying a Cyberbully

The passive-aggressive nature of cyberbullying makes it a challenge to patrol. Sometimes it involves something as seemingly harmless as a child's away message on IM that makes a veiled derogatory reference to a fellow classmate or former friend. Oftentimes, these exchanges go back and forth for a couple of hours or days, and then blow over. But when they don't, your child may be dealing with a cyberbully.

Encourage your kids to become observers of bullying tactics. It may take some time for them to understand it, but they'll be less likely to lash out in response to cyberbullying if they know what it's about. Bullies have a tendency to be obsessive in their methods, so the longer your kids observe their tactics, the easier they may become to spot.

(Note: If your child is the victim of online bullying, the bully will more than likely be a preteen, teenager, or young adult. Sexual predators tend to be over the age of twenty-five and use a far more persuasive and seductive method of grooming their victims before attempting to arrange a meeting.)

---

been a former friend who'd recently grown distant from her. In a situation like this, many parents want to take action to try to find the perpetrator and bring her to justice. But it's often a case of things easier said than done.

Another girl, this one thirteen, was forced to take action against a few cyberbullies after she discovered hateful messages posted about her on a popular social networking Web site. She wound up severing her ties with that site altogether and redis-covered the joy of talking on the phone to kids who were real friends, not just Internet acquaintances.

WHEN NAME-CALLING BECOMES BULLYING—AND THEN SOME

Taunting, teasing, and name-calling are a rather unfortunate rite of passage in adolescence. Occasionally, however, the verbal jousting can get more intense as other kids get involved, even though they don't really know what the original argument was about. This kind of mob mentality is all too common among high school and middle school students. In these types of situations, it's especially important for your kids to make sure they're docu-menting *all* of the IMs, away messages, and profiles making ref-erence to this dialog. It's not that difficult to do, and it can prove to be invaluable if it's ever necessary to bring authorities into the matter.

These days, though, cyberbullies are using more than just words to harass their victims. Advances in video technology have made it much easier for amateur moviemakers to share their work with the world through what are known as "viral videos." Virtually anyone with a camera or camera phone can make a video nowadays and post it on a Web site. So-called "viral" sites such as YouTube.com and GoogleVideo make it easy to not only post and view videos, but also to push them along to friends.

To be fair, sometimes these viral videos are completely harm-less. Many are even entertaining. Perhaps you have seen the clip of the cable TV technician who fell asleep on a customer's couch during a repair call. This video was viewed more than 500,000 times online. Funny stuff. Unfortunately for the repairman, his viral video fame didn't garner him any favor with his employer; he was fired shortly after the video was released.[4]

In the same way as the repairman's lapse of judgment made him famous online, cyberbullies often use a bit of "selective editing" on video clips to spread the unintended infamy of their targets. All it takes for a bully's rumor to seem authentic and legitimate is for him to doctor a visual. Once the clip is pushed to each member of the bully's virtual network, the infection begins to spread. And even though most reasonable adults and children can see that what's being put forth as the truth is really a lie, the visual image can leave a lasting impression in the highly influential mind of an adolescent.

ACKNOWLEDGE THE ATTACK

The conventional wisdom for dealing with teasing and name-calling used to be simple: "Sticks and stones may break my bones, but *names* will never hurt me." Here in the twenty-first century, research has proven that mean-spirited and hateful words *can* have a profoundly damaging impact on a young person's self-image. In the era of the cyberbully, it's important to do more than just try to ignore this kind of harassment.

For starters, it's wise to actually *acknowledge* that it's even taking place. Many kids don't want to believe that it could be happening to them, so they'll act as though it *isn't*. That's not a healthy way to deal with this problem either.

It's relatively easy to spot cyberbullying that involves sexually suggestive comments and other derogatory remarks. However, there are a number of other ways of harassing your child online that might seem a bit more passive on the surface but are actually far more intrusive. They include but are not limited to:

• Changing your child's password for signing on the Internet.

- Tricking your child into posting a personal secret on a Web site or IM profile.
- Printing a private or personal IM conversation without your child's knowledge or consent.
- Posting an embarrassing picture of your son or daughter or an alteration of a normal picture to give the appearance that your child is engaged in a shameful or hurtful activity.
- Visiting pornographic Web sites online while logged on to your son or daughter's account.

Each of these acts constitutes cyberbullying. If your children have *ever* experienced any of the aforementioned situations, you need to take action to stop the bullying.

WILL THE BULLYING EVER END?

Every aspect of a child's life can seem much larger to her than it really is. There's a good reason for that. Simply put, she doesn't have the perspective of many years of life to help her temper the highs and lows of daily existence. When a five-year-old says he feels like his big brother has been mean to him "all his life," he may in fact be right. For as long as this little guy has been aware of his surroundings and conscious of the presence of good and evil in the world, all he may know of his brother is continual taunting and rough-housing. And that's enough to send any kindergartener feeling as if life is *always* going to be that way.

Obviously, time provides us perspective in dealing with painful situations. But what makes the Internet such a challenge for kids who are dealing with a cyberbullying situation is the fact that what happens online can literally "go on forever." Video gaming conducted over the Internet typically has no fixed end, especially those that are known as "massively multiplayer online" games (we'll discuss these further in Chapter 9). And the same holds true for online chats, IMing, and whatever is posted onto a social networking profile. Nowadays, cyberbullies unfortunately have a multitude of means through which they can wreak havoc.

SPREADING THE HATE

A snide barb left on an IM away message can potentially be seen by each member of the accountholder's buddy list. Each of those friends could pick up on the bad vibes projected in the initial message and add additional thoughts to their own away messages. The math isn't too difficult to do: If the bully has 150 bud-

---

Believe Your Kids When They Say They're Being Bullied

It's essential that your children know you believe them when they say they're being bullied online. Assure them that you'll walk through each step of the process with them to end the attacks. Most adolescent kids usually fall into two categories when it comes to how they think their parents view them: They either think their parents don't care about them, or they figure that their parents can't possibly relate to what they're going through. But even mature adults find it difficult when they're bullied and harassed themselves. Showing your kids your own vulnerability in this area will give them a deeper sense of connection with you as you walk through this situation together.

If your children are on the receiving end of a bullying away message or bulletin, they have little if any recourse for removing it. By and large, only the profile or account holder is able to delete a bulletin posted to his or her profile. Sticks and stones may break bones . . . but a nasty away message or IM could be hanging around for quite a while. Such is the nature of the Internet.

---

dies, and each of them has an average of 150 *additional* buddies of their own . . . you can see how quickly a rumor or a hate message about just one kid can spread like wildfire.

Let's also not forget the massively popular social networking sites MySpace, Xanga, and Facebook. The typical MySpace profile holder can have literally thousands of friends, and they can post a bulletin to each of those pals that will be read by not only them but all of *their* friends—in addition to anyone who browses through and happens to run across *any* of these profiles. Remember, there are more than 100 million MySpace profiles from which to choose. That's a massive audience for some ol' fashioned hate mail.

A Never-ending Dialog

Most kids view their online communications as one long, continuous dialog. It literally goes on all day and all night nonstop. Kids leave their laptops on while they're away from them with away messages such as, "I'm having dinner with my parents—brb ['be right back']," or, "Bathroom break. Back online in 10." The reason for this never-ending connection? They don't want to be left out of the loop in case something earth-shattering goes on while they're away. (You know, like that cute guy in math class decides to IM.) In fact a healthy percentage of kids actually leave up their away messages overnight as well to inform each member on their buddy list that they're sleeping.

If this describes your child, you may need to consider restricting her Internet access. One fifteen-year-old girl had been a Xanga user for two years before switching to MySpace when she was fourteen. After breaking her curfew by thirty minutes after going to the movies one Friday evening, her mother came up with an unusual grounding. Whenever she was away from her computer, her daughter was required to leave the same away message for an entire week.

The message simply read, "I'm away from my computer right now. If you'd like to talk to me, please call." It was a revelation for her daughter. "I didn't realize how much time I put into making sure all my online friends knew exactly where I was," she remarked. "I had actually lost touch with a couple of really good friends from middle school because we used to talk all the time on the phone—until I went on MySpace." Now both mother and daughter report that the girl's social networking time has decreased significantly.

Having real, solid relationships is a great way to establish a support system that can withstand any attack by a bully, cyber or otherwise. Encourage your kids to develop and maintain the kind of authentic friendships that will build them up even when others might try to tear them down.

❧

Internet Protect Your Kids from Cyberbullies by:

1. Cautioning them not to engage with or retaliate against a cyberbully.
2. Saving any e-mail and IM communication they have with the bully.
3. Teaching them to recognize flame mail when they see it. (Simply save and file.)
4. Encouraging them to become observers of bullying tactics.
5. Believing them when they say they're being bullied online.

Chapter 7

RECOGNITION ON DEMAND: HOW THE INTERNET FEEDS YOUR CHILD'S DESIRE FOR "INSTANT" FAME, FORTUNE, AND FREEDOM

The quintessential karaoke singer used to haunt the local restaurant lounge or distant relative's wedding reception in search of an audience and a place to perform. He doesn't have to anymore. Taking the YouTube and GarageBand.com concept one step further, start-ups like KSolo and SingShot are betting that virtual Karaoke clubs will create a demand for Web sites where anyone with a modem, a Webcam, thick skin, and the sincere belief in their own talent can be a singing star.[1]

In the summer of 2002, Generation @ got its own television show.

Amateur singers in their late teens and early twenties from all across the country auditioned for the opportunity to be among the finalists vying for a recording contract from a major American record label. Each week, three celebrity judges representing different areas of the music industry sat on a panel offering encouragement and constructive criticism for the contestants. But, in the end, it was the vote of the viewing audience that determined who would be crowned champion.

The program was based on a British television show, but when *American Idol* was launched in the States, it struck a powerful nerve with audiences of all ages—especially the MySpace Generation.

Granted, the concept for *American Idol* wasn't all that different from Ed McMahon's *Star Search* series from the 1980s. Talented but unknown young performers would vie for their shot at stardom, and viewers like us would root alongside them, hoping for a bit of vicarious fame for ourselves in the process.

Occasionally a *Star Search* winner or contestant would be able to use the show as a springboard to a Hollywood career. But for the most part, we the audience were just satisfied with the process and the fact that someone was getting a shot at the big time. They were taking it, and make it or not, we as a society were collectively okay with the fact that the opportunity was all that mattered.

Fast-forward to the twenty-first century and you'll discover that America is far less patient with that "star-making" process today. In fact, one of the more highly entertaining aspects of *American Idol* is watching these young dreamers audition for the judging panel in hopes of receiving an invitation to Hollywood to actually be a part of the program.

A couple of dozen actual contestants are drawn from a pool numbering in the tens of thousands who audition. But what hooks viewers from the first moment of the first episode of each new season is watching to see which contestants can really sing—and which ones only *think* they can.

WHO'S GOT "TALENT"?

As recently as a generation ago, true talent was easy to spot. Most everyone could recognize a gifted singer, athlete, or writer. Many tried their hands at disciplines like these, yet only a few prevailed. But this generation is different. Generation @ has been brought up with heaps of praise and the expectation that the road to stardom has their name on it. As a result, many of the *Idol* hopeful who *do* wind up on the program do so only because their audition process is a reminder of what talent does *not* sound like.

But perhaps the real reason that the show is perfect for the under-twenty-five set is the fact that it gives wannabes the impression that the road to fame begins and ends on the *Idol* soundstage. Generation @ doesn't have to pay its dues like previous generations before them. Their presence, expressed desire, and natural ability are all they need to not only break into the industry, but to become hugely successful—or so they believe.

While this can be fairly harmless and even a bit entertaining on a program like *American Idol,* what happens if this line of thinking permeates other areas of a young person's life? The reality is that it *does*. Take dating, for example. The whole "courting" process is, for the most part, a thing of the past (though it still does exist in isolated pockets). Instead, many kids view dating as an excuse to get together with a member of the opposite sex and see what kind of sexual chemistry they might have with each other. With this reasoning, why not just skip the "dating" part and move right on ahead to physical intimacy?

Sadly, social networking Web sites can be used to facilitate this type of behavior.

"Consumer Sex" Online[2]

Check the "Romance and Relationships" subheading in the "Groups" category on MySpace.com and you'll see that the two most popular groups are called "Sexy Live Webcams Room" and "Sexi Kitten Group." The "kittens" signed up 30,000 members during its first week in existence, while the "Webcam" group drew more than 93,000 during the same time period.[3] Don't think teens and preteens are a part of those massive numbers? Think again.

What's more, teens are using the "personals" sections on these social networking sites to arrange "hookups" for sex with their online friends, some of whom they know but most of whom are complete strangers. Oftentimes, kids don't have to resort to advertisements, as they can communicate through IMing or simply using cyberslang (for example, many parents are unaware that to "hook up" with someone now means to have sex).

The point in mentioning this seedy online behavior is simply this: Kids have the idea that they are somehow entitled to instant gratification without waiting or, worse yet, without ramifications such as enduring hardship along the way. Want sex without dating? Find it online—it's everywhere. Want to play through a video game without having to spend all those hours failing to complete a level over and over again? Find the cheat codes or walkthrough guide online.

So where exactly did our kids get this notion? You guessed it: *us.* We are the parents who have simultaneously overindulged and neglected our children with the idea that consumerism leads to satisfaction. And this is no where more evident than in the direct-access nature of the Internet.

PRODUCER-GENERATED CONTENT

If you're a parent right now, you were born into a world where information was *delivered* to your home. Television news anchors like Walter Cronkite told your parents what happened on Capitol Hill and on Wall Street that day, while field reporters like Dan Rather literally showed them live images of the fighting in Vietnam. The morning and evening editions of local newspapers filled in the gaps of community and sporting events in a similarly unobtrusive way, since every form of delivery was available to them at their discretion. If they so chose, they could keep it from ever entering their home simply by electing whether or not to subscribe to a newspaper or by not turning on the television for the evening news. Media remained "outside."

As you grew into your teen and young adult years, however, media penetration in the home became even greater. Satellite-delivered cable television created more broadcast opportunities for media outlets, computer modems linked you to the outside world . . . and soon the world became a much smaller place.

Few of us ever had any real influence on what was reported in the media. Instead, we bought a newspaper and read about what was happening in the world around us. We watched news reports and entertainment on television. We purchased tickets

---

Establish a Policy of Privacy
When drafting your family's Internet Usage Agreement (see Appendix A), make family privacy one of your primary concerns. God established the family as one of the closest representations of heaven here on earth, and it's up to us to treat it with respect. At HomeWord our primary mission is "Encouraging Parents and Building Families," and part of that building process involves the discretion to keep certain family matters within the family. Treat your use of the Internet in the same way, respecting your own God-given institution.

---

and saw a movie or live theater. We happily consumed recorded music and baseball cards and sugary desserts and comic books and action figures and . . . all things we didn't really need but enjoyed anyway. We were "media consumers," and it's safe to say that our generation turned this passion into an art form. In all our consumerist glory, we adapted a single motto: You only use what someone else produces.

KIDS AND "USER-GENERATED" CONTENT

Now here we are raising the next generation. Only, these days kids and young adults don't share that "consumer only" mentality. They've grown up in an era when *America's Funniest Home*

Cultivate a Biblical Worldview in Your Home

There's an interesting paradox in the church today. On one side, there seems to be a large number of kids who are really passionate about their faith. They're getting involved in mission projects and community outreach. They understand that life isn't just about them, and they go all out in serving God and making a difference in this world.

You probably know some kids like that—quite a few, in fact. And yet these teens are still in the minority. Recent studies show that only one-third of the "Mosaic" or "Millennial" generation (kids born after 1984) will attend church this weekend.[4] At the same time, research also tells us that even the churchgoing kids will struggle with their faith once they reach their twenties.[5] Have you ever wondered what will help those kids return to their first love and start a new season of following the Lord once again? The same thing that will keep them from making poor decisions online: a biblical worldview.

Kids in twenty-first century America have been brought up in a "values-neutral" culture. It has no moral absolutes, and kids have been taught that all truth is relative based on individual experience.

Likewise, the Internet is values-neutral. It does not distinguish between good and evil, or right and wrong. It's merely a place where content is created and then distributed, where ideas are presented and then accepted, rejected, or ignored. It's a perfect match for the under-twenty-five set, as amoral a collective of individuals as our society has ever seen.

Now more than ever it is essential for us as parents to cultivate a biblical worldview in our homes. Simply put, a person who views the Bible as containing the guidelines for right living holds a biblical worldview. Teaching your kids that there are moral absolutes gives them security in a "whatever" world, and it will go a long way toward Internet Protecting Your Kids as well.

Videos was a television constant. Their parents—that would be *us*—have been chasing them around with camcorder in hand since the moment they were born, recording as many of their waking moments as our video tapes and memory cards would hold. These kids have been involved in more video projects in their brief adolescent years than many major movie actors are throughout their entire careers.

It makes sense, then, that members of this younger generation see themselves not only as consumers of media but also *producers* of it as well. For as long as they can remember, they've been the stars of their own shows. As a result, what makes the Internet so appealing to them is the fact that it provides them with what they crave: a place to put their lives on display for as many of their peers (and others) as possible.

I Always Feel Like Somebody's Watching Me

This concept of "audience as entertainment" without the need for a script has been percolating in our culture for some time now. It came full-fledge with the rise of so-called "reality TV" and such shows as *Survivor* and *Big Brother*. Now it's transi-

---

Establish an Online Playlist

The adolescent years are marked by both positive peer influence as well as negative peer pressure. How your kids respond to both will speak volumes about both their character and their self-image. If your son hears others at school, youth group, or soccer practice talking about a certain Web site, you can be certain his curiosity will be aroused. The question is, What will his next step be? Visit the site and check it out for himself? What happens if it turns out to be a pornographic Web site?

Your job as a parent is to proactively anticipate this potential dilemma and then provide a solution for your children before it confronts them. That's why it's helpful to actually rehearse what could happen before they respond. Make this an ongoing dialog with your kids about the harmful kinds of Web sites they might encounter. Help them to see what the outcome might be if they visit such a site. And be sure to include the "Mom and Dad" factor. Let them know in no uncertain terms that, if they have a question about a site they want to check out, they should check it out with you first. You'll spare your kids from a lot of unnecessary anxiety if you stay approachable for questions like these.

---

tioned, for the most part, away from the tightly-scripted and edited network shows to an Internet-based YouTube world in which two guys with a camcorder can share the same fifteen minutes of fame as a reality TV star.

Now, there's really nothing wrong with a couple of buddies taking their skateboards and a video camera to a local skatepark and having one of them record the action while the other tries to do amazing tricks. Their exploits will no doubt wind up on someone's MySpace page, where the whole world can witness streaming video of what may or may not turn out to be an exercise in "shredding." The real danger lies in the fact that these kids can create this homemade video and make it available to more than 100 million Internet users *directly*, never realizing that a few of those who view it might be the kind of people they would not willingly associate with in real life. Yet the truth is, they just did by making a connection online.

A major difference between media presentation in the past and the present is knowing who assumes responsibility for protecting the end user—those of us who view the material—from any potentially damaging after-effects. A generation ago, the content provider assumed liability. These days, however, that burden falls squarely on *our* shoulders.

DIRECT ACCESS ONLINE

As we've already seen, venturing online involves both remarkable positives and nightmarish negatives. Another example of this is the fact that the Internet gives its users direct access to those who pontificate their views virtually without context. While this is not inherently bad, it does mean that the consumer himself is the only "filter" of sorts available to help process these views and opinions expressed online. Noted talk-show host Hugh Hewitt is an authority on the rise of online journals, also known as "Web logs" or "blogs." He points out that the Internet has led to the "disintermediation of information in our culture." In other words, going online gives each of us direct access to the news and information we need *without* interference from a "middle man."[6]

This can work to our advantage in many areas of life: researching for projects, reconnecting with old friends from school, getting real-time stock quotes, traffic reports, or weather forecasts. But it can also lead to kids wanting and subsequently *expecting* direct connection to the source of information or connection they're seeking. And should that connection turn out to be a bad influence, your son or daughter could wind up another "camkid" using a Webcam and a PayPal account to operate his own porn site.

LIFE ON DEMAND

At this point you might be breathing a sigh of relief and muttering under your breath, "Whew, that was a close one. Good thing *my* kids would never want to get involved with something that horrible." The truth is, while your children may not be surfing the Web *actively looking* for bad influences, their worldview is being shaped by a subtle yet consistent message in the culture that they *can* actually control their own environment. This mindset leaves many kids extremely vulnerable to attacks from predators simply because they honestly have no concept that anyone other than a friend or family member could *ever* have direct access to them online.

If you *still* don't think your kids could be at risk, consider the "on-demand" attitude most children have toward electronic communication in general:

> 1. Internet-based phone services such as Vonage give kids and young adults a sense of direct connection without phone company assistance. This attitude plays into the false sense of security children develop from the "invisible invincibility" they think they have

online as well. There are currently nearly twenty million subscribers to this kind of service internationally, and the number of users in the U.S. has quadrupled over the past twelve months.[7]

2. "Buddy lists" and instant messaging enable kids and young adults to see which of their friends is currently online and then to connect with them immediately if they are available. Instant access has become an unspoken online right, particularly for kids.

3. "Push to talk" (or PTT) phones provide users with the same type of buddy list for their cell phones. A caller's phone number is entered into the address book and then highlighted whenever that person's phone is active, giving callers instant access by phone to that person. Caller ID—now a staple on most phones—also lets them know who is calling so they don't have to actually ever remember the phone number. This process also makes it possible for kids to avoid the now-horribly outdated process of practicing proper phone etiquette. They're made aware of exactly who is calling in and are never burdened with not being able to connect with someone who is not readily available.

4. Internet blogs give bloggers the opportunity to connect via an online message board. Blogs are also prominent fixtures on social networking sites such as MySpace.

5. Camera phones with wireless connections enable users to push photos or video streams directly to Web sites, e-mail addresses, or other cell phones. News

organizations are now encouraging viewers to upload videos of breaking news so they can include them on their television newscasts and Web sites.

EDUCATION = PREVENTION AND PROTECTION

While none of these features is bad in and of itself, each can still leave an Internet user potentially vulnerable to exposure from unwanted influences. No longer are your children simply susceptible to getting mixed in with a couple of bad apples at school. Now they could link up with potentially *hundreds of thousands* of negative influencers within seconds. Consider the fact that during 2006, when 20th Century Fox created a MySpace page to

---

Learn How Your Kids Communicate with Their Friends
During adolescence, your kids still need your influence as a parent, but they'll also lean heavily on the opinions of their friends. That's why it's helpful to do a "communications audit" of all the ways your children connect with their friends. Whether it's through instant messaging, cell phone, or text messaging, determine the one they use most often. Then make it a point to use that method at least once a week as your primary means of keeping in touch with your kids. You may have to brush up on your text-messaging skills or IM lingo to make this work, but you can do it! Make the effort to reach out to your kids in language they understand.

---

promote the movie *X-Men: The Last Stand*, it attracted more than three million friends to the site. It's frightening to realize this is now the sphere of influence in which every child roams.

Obviously, you can't monitor every single action your children take online. But you *can* take steps to educate them so they can make right and wise decisions. And you can also take precautions to help safeguard their actions when they do make the occasional misstep of youth. Be the change you hope to instill in your kids.

Internet Protect Your Kids from Unnecessary Exposure Online by:

1. Establishing a "Policy of Privacy" with regard to the kind of personal family information shared online.
2. Cultivating a biblical worldview in the lives of your kids that helps them learn discretion and encourages a desire to live for something greater than temporary "fame."
3. Rehearsing the consequences of putting private and personal information on display online.
4. Recognizing that even good and smart kids are prone to make foolish choices regarding what they post online.
5. Educating your kids about the benefits of making right and wise decisions online.

Chapter 8

CONNECTING WITH KIDS: WHY THE INTERNET IS THEIR FIRST CHOICE FOR COMMUNICATION

Dan was the kind of dad every kid liked having around. He loved working with children, whether he was coaching his son's Little League team or helping with his daughter's high school group at church. Dan was outgoing in a laid-back sort of way, so he never had to work too hard to get the kids he worked with to open up to him.

That's why it hit him so hard when he noticed some rather dramatic changes in his daughter Taryn's personality. "The moment she started high school, it was like she became a completely different person," Dan said. "She's always been pretty independent, so when she started to pull away a bit, I figured that was normal. But then she went from being really outgoing to totally quiet and withdrawn. I couldn't figure out what was wrong."

Dan talked to a couple of other parents about how to find answers to his questions. When one of them suggested looking at Taryn's MySpace profile, Dan realized that he didn't even know how to access her account.

We can learn a lot from Dan's example. If he wanted to find

out what was really going on in his daughter's life, he was probably going to do so by reading her blogs, listening to her music
samples, and checking out the pictures she had posted on her
online profile. When he did, Dan discovered that his "outgoing"
fourteen-year-old honor student was actually struggling with
school for the first time in her life. Her grades were suffering, she
wasn't sure if she was going to make the soccer team, and she was
having a hard time making friends. Taryn was hurting, so she
reached out to the people she hoped could give her immediate
help: her online friends who she felt were like a family to her.

PUSHING AND PULLING[1]

Dan's attempts to reach out to his daughter and Taryn's reaction
to a difficult first few weeks in high school provide us with a
snapshot of a fundamental difference between parents and kids
in how we view using the Internet. It's a matter of "push" versus
"pull." Here's how it works:

When you sit down at your computer, what do you see when
you look at the screen? Pictures from your last vacation? A quote

---

Put It in Writing

Kids who spend a lot of time online feel as comfortable writing out
a text message, e-mail, or IM dialog as they do having an actual conversation in person or over the phone. So why not go "old school" on
your children and use a handwritten note to connect with them at
least once a week?

The majority of parents who contact the HomeWord radio
broadcast share with us the power their words of affirmation have in
the lives of their children. You'd be amazed how much influence you
can have in your kids' lives by doing something as simple as giving
them a scripture verse on a three-by-five card with a note expressing your love. It doesn't have to be deeply personal or terribly profound, but sharing your feelings and your hopes and dreams for your
children in writing will have a profound impact on improving the
communication between you and your children.

What Kids Reveal About Themselves Online
Southern Californian organization TeenWatch conducted a survey based on a random sampling of kids with MySpace accounts. It found that a staggering 90 percent of them have included the following items in either their blogs or personal profiles on at least two occasions: their personal cell phone numbers, IM screen names, personal e-mail addresses, even the directions to their homes. What's more shocking is the fact that so many of these kids actually leave that information on their profiles indefinitely.[2]

that keeps you going on exceptionally long work days? Reminders of the growing number of e-mail messages you still need to return?

If you're like most adults, you view your computer as a means to an end. It's a tool for helping you accomplish tasks such as finding directions, stock quotes, sports scores, or the headlines of the day. Once you get what you need, you'll "grab" it and go. You *pull*. No questions asked, no further explanation necessary. There's no need for small talk or relationship-building with your computer. It is a machine, after all.

If you want to be able to *Internet Protect Your Kids*, however, you have to understand what your children experience when they go online. To them, the Internet *is* their reality. They view their online activity as a vehicle to connect with new friends and to build community with the kids they already know (emphasis on *friends* and not on *parents*). In other words, they *push*. During the middle school and high school years, it's a healthy and normal thing for children to want to move from dependence on us as parents to independence. And social networking sites like MySpace, Xanga, and Facebook give them the opportunity to pursue that sense of independence. The fact that there are more than 150 million registered profiles between those sites is a clear indication that the demand for online socializing is high, especially in light of the realization that nearly one-third of those users are under the age of twenty-five.[3]

NO ONE IS ANONYMOUS ONLINE

What our kids don't realize is that in the midst of connecting with new and old online acquaintances, they remain constantly exposed. It is *impossible* to log onto and browse the Web anonymously. Every click is being carefully scrutinized by *someone*, whether it's the operator of a search engine tracking the categories or keywords being searched, or the spammer who's attaching cookies (Web site markers showing where you've visited) or spyware (hidden online tracking software) to your e-mail

---

Getting the Message through to Our Kids

When a teen or preteen looks to an online relationship as a main source of connection, it should serve as a loud wake-up call for her parents. If that describes your situation with your own kids right now, take the steps necessary to reestablish that connection. Obviously, not all kids will seem interested in connecting with their parents. Yet children crave connection, no matter what age. And it's no secret that the relationship from which they desire it the most is the one involving Mom and Dad.

Dr. Gary Chapman, who's a regular contributor to HomeWord, has infamously identified five different "love languages" we all use to communicate: words of affirmation, gifts, quality time, acts of service, and appropriate physical touch.[4] If you're looking for a way to establish or reestablish a solid connection with your kids, unplug the computer for a moment and get to know their love language. You may have a child who loves hugs, so hug him often. If gifts get your daughter's attention, give them—but be sure to use them wisely. You get the idea.

---

address. The latter guarantees also you'll soon be hit by an endless succession of annoying pop-up advertisements. That's why it's up to us as parents to impress upon our children the reality of the online world they find so appealing. *Everything* they do online is subject to someone else's scrutiny. Even though some SNSes and chat rooms offer privacy controls, they can often be bypassed with some simple yet careful Internet maneuvering.

It's been said that parents can pour all the love, care, compassion, and common sense we can into our kids during their first twelve years of life, but once they hit middle school, they enter a season in which they forget *everything* and wind up having to learn it all again. True or not, perhaps that's a helpful attitude to take when it comes to teaching your kids how to stay safe online.

Think back to when your kids were infants and toddlers. For the most part, they were completely innocent and enjoyed the simple things in life. They were learning lessons that would become building blocks for the preschool and elementary years. Remember how easy it was to make your daughter laugh back then? Sometimes a quick game of peekaboo was all it took to do the trick. She would cover her eyes and—poof!—she'd be gone. And in her mind, *you* would disappear, too. Obviously, no one *disappeared*. But your daughter was just learning about "object permanence," and how nothing goes away just because we close our eyes or someone turns off the light in the room.

Amazingly, it isn't that different when your daughter becomes a preteen or teen. She looks at her online world as something she can control, as if covering her eyes or closing them altogether will somehow make her invisible to any potential predator. She may utilize some of the more common Internet precautions when she's online, but if she's like most kids her age, she routinely shares extremely sensitive information about her life and family online with total strangers.

I NEED TO BE HEARD!

Most researchers acknowledge that the most effective communication between two people involves 15 percent speaking and 85 percent listening. Yet every teen and preteen wants to be heard, and the online world gives them a chance to speak out with an assurance that there's someone on the other end listening. With instant messaging, this give-and-take communication is constant, easy, and instant—all elements that make it a

Internet Protect Your Daughter

If you allow your daughter to have an IM account or social networking profile, consider making one of the requirements be that she adopt a masculine-sounding screen identifier—and definitely one that does not include any part of her own name. Remember that on the Web you're under no obligation to use a proper name. Think safety when choosing online identification.

Generation @ trademark.

It was young people who led the world away from telephone conversations to sending e-mail online, so it makes sense that they're also the ones who are now abandoning e-mail in favor of the more rapid-fire IM approach. Electronic mailboxes are going the way of their metal counterparts in front of the house. Just as the junk mail pieces fill up the box at home, spam now overruns so many e-mail boxes, causing fewer and fewer young people to use them. "Besides," as one teenage boy pointed out, "e-mail is *so* much slower than IMing."

At the heart of the migration away from e-mail are kids' relationships with the adults in their world. Adolescents will typically tend to migrate *away* from their parents during the adolescent years. As adults have become more e-mail adept, their children have moved to IMing largely because their parents can't keep up. Try having five rapid-fire chats online sometime (which you can do simultaneously with IMing) and you'll see what we mean!

This shift in preference from e-mail to IMing may be a concern for some parents, but it doesn't have to be. In fact, one unexpected benefit of the IM phenomenon is that many kids are learning how to do a better job of dealing with interruptions—a skill that may serve them well once they enter the workforce.

GIRLS LEADING THE WAY . . . AGAIN

It used to be the snapshot image of an average tween or teen girl involved her lying on her bed talking on the phone for hours to her friends. That picture can officially be updated now to the world of instant messaging. Yet because girls make up the majority of IMers and chat-room users, they also run a greater risk than boys of being stalked, bullied, or receiving unwanted sexual advances online.

A recent study conducted by the University of Maryland's Center for Risk and Reliability found that female screen names generated 100 malicious messages a day, compared to an average of only four per day for male names used in this study. For the record, the gender-neutral names used in the survey attracted an average of twenty-five daily messages of a malicious nature.[5]

More than Words

The constant dialog kids and young adults are having online isn't limited to IMing, text messaging, blogs, or even chat rooms. Part of the communication process now involves music, digital photos, and video streams that can be pushed from one site to multiple others in a user's online community. Your son or daughter's site can become an entire multimedia entertainment center for his or her online friends. And words aren't even necessary for this exchange.

The technology to keep the dialog going is also becoming ever-present. Video gaming systems such as the Xbox 360™ or Sony's PlayStation Portable (PSP®) now come equipped with the means for gamers to chat online with fellow competitors while they're competing against one another. Cell phones now come "WiFi equipped," meaning users don't just have to dial a number or IM to exchange information, they now have wireless Internet access wherever they go. In addition to this, these phones provide the capacity to enter another world of fun (and possible danger): taking pictures and shooting videos.

It's no surprise that the under-twenty-five market has taken so readily to portable camera phones. While the quality isn't always as good as a photography buff would prefer, the trade-off is that young users can easily and conveniently snap a digital photo or shoot video wherever and whenever they want. Having an on-demand video production facility right inside their cell phones means that kids and young adults can afford to partake in one of their favorite indulgences—seeing themselves on-screen—with the greatest of ease.

Most of these pictures and videos are completely innocent. As stated earlier, there's nothing wrong with two buddies sending pictures of themselves to each other as a means of goofing off. But the reality is that some social networking sites have garnered

---

The School's Home Page

If your child's teachers have a page on their school or district Web site, take some time to go over it with your child. A typical school-sponsored teacher's site should include a syllabus of the coursework students will be covering during the current quarter or semester. It may also include a progress report that will give you the opportunity to encourage your child in their progress grade-wise. If your child's school does not have a Web site in place, offer to help set up one.

---

reputations as being havens for kids whose photos cross the line from playful to pornographic. And sadly, there *are* a growing number of teens and preteens who see this kind of expression as their only means for dealing with intense emotional pain. If you sense that your child might fall into that category, you may want to reconsider whether she really needs a camera phone at this time.

SCHOOLING ON THE WEB

As much time as kids spend online these days, they still spend more hours each day *on campus*. The school experience has always been and continues to be one of the single most powerful influences on the under-twenty-five set. Yet even in classrooms and lecture halls across the country the Internet is becoming a major part of the way they're being educated.

School-sponsored home pages enable instructors to keep students updated on assignments, upcoming projects, and grades. Online research is replacing actual visits to the library for research projects. Once those reports are completed, many students are required to register them through sites such as www.turnitin.com, where the content can be checked for plagiarism to reduce the chance that a student would use one of the thousands of previously written reports that are available online. Once approved by the site, the student is then free to turn in the project for actual grading.

It's worth noting at this point that instructors aren't immune from scrutiny online. Web sites such as www.ratemypro fessor.com give college students the opportunity to provide fellow classmates with their personal assessment of an instructor from classes taken in previous semesters. While both abusable and unscientific in assessing the quality of education a student gets, this word-of-mouth rating method still has its advantages for informing students about certain teachers.

In today's educational world, kids meet at school and then strengthen that connection online . . . which leads to a greater sense of community at school . . . which translates into an even stronger desire for connectivity online . . . and the cycle continues.

In the 1950s, kids used to congregate at the malt shop. In the '60s, it was at the drive-in. The '70s found kids connecting at pizza places. It was video arcades in the '80s and shopping malls in the '90s. But today kids like to hang out in virtual communities online. It's where they feed their need for connection, and it's become their primary means of communication. As parents, it's crucial that we recognize this and start speaking their language.

Internet Protect the Way Your Kids Communicate Online by:

1. Doing a "communications audit" of all the ways they communicate with their friends.
2. Using handwritten communication to express encouragement and your hopes and dreams for them at least once each week.
3. Learning each child's "love language," and then speaking it often to him or her.
4. Choosing masculine-sounding screen identifiers for instant messaging, e-mailing, and social networking profiles.
5. Familiarizing yourself with the school-sponsored teacher's Web site for their class—or volunteering to establish one if it doesn't already exist.

Chapter 9

AMUSING THEMSELVES TO DEATH? WHY THE INTERNET IS KIDS' FIRST CHOICE FOR RECREATION

Any discussion about how to *Internet Protect Your Kids* is bound to involve preventing pornography, sexual predators, or cyberbullies from harming your children. But there are many other concerns for parents regarding Internet safety. The problem is that they just don't *appear* to be problematic on the surface. For example, consider four of the major forms of recreation in the life of a teen or preteen: music, movies, television, and video games. Each of these categories presents its own set of parental challenges individually. However, what's worth noting is not so much the categories themselves but the *source* that now provides each of these media to our children: the Internet.

THE MAKINGS OF ONLINE ENTERTAINMENT

As with virtually every online trend, kids and young adults were among the first audience segment to purchase music, videos, and games from the Internet. (Legally downloading television shows is a relatively recent development, though pirating of this type was done years before.) In fact, the connection between the music industry and the online community began in simple college dorm rooms—though not with the music industry's approval. When word got to artists and record executives that there was an increasingly popular Web site allowing users to share music, it didn't take long for them to realize this not only gave people unlimited access to their music (a positive), it also came with those industry types never seeing a dime (obviously a negative). Napster.com quickly emerged as an online behemoth that the music world had to confront—or else risk its own demise. Even if you weren't tech-savvy in the mid-1990s, it was almost impossible to miss hearing about Napster. The site became the go-to place for music lovers who wanted to download all their favorite songs from the Internet but didn't feel the compulsion to pay for any of them.

The Napster concept was simple: A user would upload a song or collection of songs to the site to "share" with other users. Those users could then locate the tunes, download them onto their own computers and, if they so chose, "rip and burn" the music onto their own compilation audio CD. Finding songs on the site was as easy as using a search function. With a catalog spanning decades of music and hundreds of thousands of songs, you can see how the site quickly turned Average Joes into managers of their own private CD store. Is it any wonder music sales began to suffer?

FOLLOWING OUR EXAMPLE?

If this behavior sounds somewhat criminal to you, remember that it wasn't that long ago that many of the owners of vinyl LP records and blank audio cassettes engaged in a similar practice during the 1970s and '80s.

As expected, the music industry howled because of the copyright infringement and the unlawful reproduction of artists' work, and Napster in its original form folded shop in July 2001 after a lengthy court battle. Yet the site's prominence in culture—and especially among a younger generation—awoke the music industry to the reality that there was a large and growing market for purchasing music online. It became evident that people were no longer as interested in trekking down to a local record store to browse through or buy music. They wanted what they wanted, and they wanted it when they wanted it. Rather than trying to squelch this newfound demand, the industry wisely sought to capitalize on it. The venture almost instantly proved successful, as evidenced by the rise in popularity of sites such as Apple's iTunes and the burgeoning market for portable MP3 players.

In many ways, we've come full circle in the music industry, with downloads of individual songs selling for relatively the same price as the old 45-rpm "singles" of a few generations ago. Those of us who grew up in that era might have enjoyed a few glorious moments each day spinning our favorite tunes on a simple phonograph. But the kids and young adults of today utilize songs as if they comprised a soundtrack for the story of their lives. Generation @ has immersed itself in a never-ending set list of tunes. And considering kids' propensity to want to archive each waking moment either in pixel or blog form, music takes on an even bigger role.

TOO MUCH OF A GOOD THING?

The fact that kids can spend exorbitant amounts of time searching out, listening to, and then purchasing new music online can be problematic in and of itself for parents. Most teens and pre-teens can talk for hours on end about their favorite musical groups. The Internet provides them with the opportunity to do just that via chat rooms, online forums, and even the bands' own Web sites. This gives kids that *direct connection* with the artists and other fans that they so desperately crave—which can be a distinctly positive experience. At the same time, however, there's a decidedly greater risk that children may wander astray online simply by pursuing "more of a good thing" when it comes to the music they enjoy.

Think of the following common scenario: A teenage boy favors hard rock music over any other style. He goes online to browse the sites of a couple of his favorite bands and decides to purchase a few of their songs or entire albums. In the process of finalizing his purchase, he's redirected to another site where he can complete the transaction. Once there, he spots a few customer reviews of the project he's about to buy that are listed below.

The reviews he reads include a couple of recommendations to check out other bands that are "way better" than the group he's familiar with. So he uses a popular search engine to find out more about these other bands and winds up being linked to a pornographic, profanity-laden chat room claiming to be a "forum" where one of these other bands' music is being discussed.

Such is the way it can go on the Internet. Sadly, a well-intentioned, music-loving fifteen-year-old is always potentially just one click away from heading down an online path to destruction.

TWO SIDES TO EVERY COIN

At this point it's worth mentioning yet again how one of the major *blessings* the Internet brings can also be an unimaginable *burden* to parents at times. The ability to seek information online gives users far greater access to more helpful resources than ever before. At its finest, the Internet is a private Library of Congress placed in every home. At the same time, the downside of this immense and virtually infinite resource is that those same users—who are seeking out positive, helpful information—can just as easily (and often unknowingly) be exposed to an unprecedented amount of harmful, pornographic content. As wonderful and beneficial as the Internet is, parents must always remember that without safety precautions, it remains a double-edged sword.

Get Other Parents Involved

There is wisdom in the counsel of many (see Proverbs 15:22), and parenting your kids through their entertainment choices is one area of life where wisdom should definitely prevail. If you're eager to receive godly counsel from other parents who have "been there" before, consider starting a blog or MySpace profile and invite experienced parents you know to post reviews of current movies they've seen, music they've listened to, video games they've played, etc. Prompt them to explain the reasons why they did or did not choose to allow their kids to experience a particular piece of entertainment.

You could also offer to organize and/or host a "Family Media Night" in your home. Parents could join you in your home for a night where a few movies/albums/video games/etc. could be reviewed, followed by a discussion of how your kids would benefit from seeing them. If that proves successful, you could eventually make this a real family affair, allowing your kids to also participate by bringing in a movie, music CD, or video game they've discovered to have some family benefit. The kids will feel affirmed for bringing choices approved by their parents ahead of time to the event, and parents can learn from each other about acceptable movies, music, and video games that come with a built-in endorsement from other parents they can trust.

In the more traditional "brick and mortar" era of retail, such pornographic content and negative influences were much easier to avoid. For example, in the past, a local record store would have had all its music on display. Songs containing obscenities were certainly never played in-store, nor were they allowed on the radio or TV. In fact, artists who ventured into crude territory almost immediately felt the ramifications since most music retailers wouldn't risk wasting shelf space on them in their stores.

As culture has shifted and our music has continued to push the boundaries, what was before blacklisted has now become mainstream. Obviously, this has made parents' jobs of protecting their children from harmful musical influences difficult. With the Internet, however, that task becomes even harder. A retailer has virtually unlimited storage for the albums he'll sell—which means consumers have an equally extensive catalog at their disposal. In addition, obscenity is far less of an issue due to an absence of laws prohibiting it online. Those two facts alone can make the online music experience a harrowing one, both for kids as well as their parents.

THE MYSPACE CONNECTION

As we mentioned in Chapter 2, music played a key role in the inception of the Web's most influential site, MySpace. Co-founder Tom Anderson is a musician who enlisted the help of his good friend and Internet "techie" Chris DeWolfe to establish a site where college students could showcase up-and-coming musical artists with whom their friends might not be familiar. The young men intended for their site to be all about people connecting over music.

As word about the site spread, its popularity grew. Anderson and DeWolfe continued to fuel that growth by giving users the tools they needed to blog about musical acts and upload MP3s and video clips. From those relatively modest beginnings, MySpace has emerged as one of the most powerful influences on our culture in terms of the promotion of music, movies, and other forms of entertainment media. It's rare now for a new movie or album to be released without being linked in advertisements to its promotional MySpace page. Artists, recording studios and movie studios frequently make songs, clips, and promotional material available on the site so users can push those items to their online friends. Concert information and other music news is also available to fans of these artists. In short, MySpace has become *the* place for any emerging entertainment to establish a fan base.

A FIRSTHAND ENCOUNTER

It's another packed house on a sultry Thursday evening at the Plush Club in the heart of Fullerton, California. One of the locals estimates the crowd at around 150 or so, even though this "club" is nothing more than an oversized coffee house that actually should hold half as many.

A few minutes before show time, I (Roger) meet up with my fifteen-year-old daughter, who had already arrived with a half-dozen or so of her friends from school. High school and college-age kids have been making "Plush Thursdays" the place to be for as long as many of them can remember. They first found out about this regular affair online on artist Tyrone Wells' MySpace page.

After a couple of opening acts finish their sets, Tyrone takes the stage. He is tall and thin with a shaved head and an easygoing demeanor that has begun to attract quite a following. Tonight's crowd is with him from the first chord of his opening number, and they thoroughly enjoy every moment of his set. They can sing all of his songs by heart. They've heard every story he uses to introduce each song, but they *still* laugh in all the right places.

After the show, they'll amble over to the product table in the back of the club and snap up the merchandise available: Tyrone's CDs—four of them (all independently produced)—along with an assortment of T-shirts and posters. He'll hang around and sign a few autographs and pose for pictures with adoring fans, who all seem to have created a Tyrone Wells "photo album" on their cell phones. They'll run home and e-mail those images to all their friends later that night. They thoroughly enjoyed the show, as did I—even if I was one of only about three people over the age of thirty in the entire place.

"MAKING IT" THROUGH MYSPACE

Tyrone Wells is one of countless local artists struggling for recognition on the national level, but he has developed a local core audience through hard work, strategic perseverance . . . and a profile on MySpace.com.

"I've had a Web site for most of my career," he told me after the concert, "but when we started to utilize MySpace, it enabled our fans to take even more ownership in what we were doing. It gave them the ability to be actively involved in promoting, critiquing, and commenting on my music."

Judging by the fan reaction at this concert, Tyrone's supporters have become more than just fans; they're his *friends*. "[MySpace] is a great tool for me to be more connected with my audience."

The "Plush Thursday" show was no exception. His fans saw the show promoted on his MySpace page, and that was all they needed to know. It didn't matter that most of them had never heard of the venue before. Besides, this could be their last opportunity to catch him in concert for a while. He was about to head off on a tour of the East Coast that would hit close to 100 college campuses and span nearly eight months. He was playing a show at the House of Blues in nearby Los Angeles the following week, but that show had been sold out for some time.

CONTROLLING THE CROWD

Having a presence on MySpace can be a tremendous boost for a musician struggling for recognition. But maintaining that presence can be a tremendous challenge. That's why Mark Chipelo is such a valuable member of the Tyrone Wells team. Mark accompanies Tyrone onstage playing a box drum called a "cajon," an odd hybrid of a kick drum and tambourine. He also handles all of the event booking, in addition to being Webmaster for Tyrone's MySpace page.

"It does take a lot of work," Mark says, "but it's such a great way to interact with the kids who are supporting us right now. It's my job to make sure that the comments they post are appropriate. If they aren't, I take them down right away." Appropriate or not, online buzz is something every artist wants. And the viral marketing that MySpace provides to such acts as Tyrone Wells is invaluable. Make no mistake, the music industry is taking notice.

Record executives can track the progress of promising talent. The artist establishes a profile that includes particulars such as bio information and upcoming concert dates. Music can also be uploaded onto the profile and other MySpace account holders can listen to the songs for free. The record labels can then track the number of times each song has been played off of the profile and how many page views the profile received. They can even see the kinds of comments fans are posting about the music that's included on the profile.

In the case of Tyrone, the MySpace presence is paying off. On a recent trip to New York he met with Avery Lipman, the senior vice president of Universal Republic Records. Lipman noted that his own first exposure to Tyrone's music was through his MySpace page. After tracking his progress there for some time, Tyrone signed with Lipman's label. Undeniably, the invaluable exposure to millions of users via MySpace paved the way.

Don't Trust the Ratings

Oftentimes, the current system for rating movies does little to take into account your values as a parent. The inconsistency of the Motion Picture Association of America (MPAA), a panel of movie-goers that does the rating, can be downright frustrating. That's why you'll want to do all you can to educate yourself about what's playing in theaters right now. These are the movies your kids and their friends will likely want to see this weekend. Avoid the possibility of your children being blindsided by questionable or offensive content that could never get mentioned in a simple ratings letter. Stay current and continue to be a student of their culture.

Focus on the Family's Plugged In helps you do exactly this without you having to screen every movie that's out there. Offered both in a print magazine and online format, Plugged In offers reviews, feature stories, cultural trend analysis, "Family Movie Night" guides, and much more. In addition to a comprehensive library of past and current movie reviews, this excellent resource also covers music, television, and video games. For more information, check out www.pluggedinonline.com.

THE ONLINE MOVIE EXPERIENCE

Though music was essentially the first form of online entertainment to capture the attention of the under-twenty-five set, it's certainly not the only one. The motion picture industry is now benefiting from a "best of both worlds" attitude currently prevailing in the minds of consumers.

Almost all personal computers now come equipped with DVD technology that makes it possible to watch movies at home or on the road. Likewise, portable DVD players and video iPods also make long road trips a bit easier for kids (and their parents) to bear. As a result of a recent home-theater frenzy, many families now opt to stay in, rent a movie and experience it with theater-like sound and visuals—thanks to powerful surround-sound speakers and sixty-inch plasma or LCD televisions. On those rare occasions when consumers do venture out of the house for visual entertainment, they'll find countless choices for their viewing pleasure at the local cinema.

What's unique about the movie experience at present is that each aspect can begin *online*. Tickets for the multiplex show can be purchased in advance on a site like www.fandango.com and then printed out once you arrive at the theater. Should you choose to "order in" a movie, you can either utilize a digital on-demand feature, rent a DVD online through a company like NetFlix, or download a copy of a movie and then burn it onto a DVD directly from your home computer, courtesy of a company like CinemaNow.[1]

All these advances in modern technology may make it easier for us to watch first-run movies in our homes, but only if the content matches our values. Film critic and media analyst Michael Medved has written extensively about the motion picture industry's unwillingness to fully embrace the family audience. In his book *Hollywood vs. America,* he notes the obvious benefits to society that classic "family" movies bring. But then he goes a step further, noting the profitability factor as well.

According to Medved's research, the average G-rated film typically returns $25 million for every $10 million spent to produce and market the project. That's a solid 250 percent return on investment that any businessperson would readily welcome![2] And yet by and large, studios are set on releasing more PG-13 movies than any other category. The reason? It's perceived that teenagers feel G- and PG-rated movies are too "childish" for them, while they obviously shouldn't be attending R-rated ones (though the latter issue—and how it relates to studio's marketing tactics—is anther conversation in and of itself).

The result is that Hollywood, by the numbers, produces far more movies *unsuitable* for families than not. Granted, in recent years, the motion picture industry has made some positive strides in this area, as families are speaking out by their absence at the box office. As a result, more "family friendly" content is being produced, which gives us as parents more and better choices regarding what kinds of movies we'll let our children watch.

THE ELEPHANT IN THE ROOM

We parents have shown tremendous concern over the kinds of movies that are marketed to our children. And we've stood in the gap on their behalf with regards to music, TV shows, and magazines that have pushed the decency envelope. But there's an industry that's now dwarfing all of these others—and yet we've done little if anything to even acknowledge its presence, let alone its power. Despite colossal earnings, the video game industry has remained the elephant in the room that we know exists but have chosen to ignore. Yet if we hope to *Internet Protect Our Kids*, we can ignore it no longer. Video gaming is one of the fastest growing segments of the entertainment industry, and the Internet is playing a vital role in fueling its demand.

If you've been to a video rental store recently you've probably noticed the emergence of video games. Over the past few years, games have begun to take up more and more shelf space, while movie rentals go the way of the Web. In fact, many movie rental stores have been replaced by shops offering new and used video games for rent or purchase. Sales of new video game titles now outsell those of movies on DVD. The strong resale market of these titles keeps these businesses going strong, and the

---

Something for Nothing?

Before we go any further, take a word of advice about "free" offers from any entertainment company online. Kids are often lured into dangerous areas online by offers of free entertainment pieces such as music or movie downloads. Sometimes these are legitimate offers from reputable companies. But often they are little more than come-ons from less-than-reputable organizations looking to spread a computer virus or link your computer to pornography.

It's worth noting that some social networking sites do make provisions for artists to provide free clips of their music. Those sites are monitored by the Web host, and postings/offers/freebies that no longer meet the site's criteria are removed immediately. Brief two-minute clips from popular television programs are also sometimes offered online without cost, as are some original online-only series. Many of these "mobisodes" have become quite popular. Be forewarned, however, that from time to time they may push the envelope with risqué content, violence, or mild language.

Internet works in seamless harmony with print media and the traditional establishments in getting that job done.

One of the biggest factors contributing to those impressive sales numbers is online gaming. The technology behind gaming has come a long way since the days of the penny arcade. Now millions of gamers can simultaneously sharpen their skills going head-to-head with fellow Internet competitors all over the world. There are a number of different ways an online gamer can engage in Internet combat. The most common of these are titles known as "massively multiplayer online games," or MMOGs.

These mammoth games consist of virtual worlds where thousands of people can play at the same time. Each player has the potential to interact with others while playing the game on his own. The typical MMO gamer is an eighteen- to thirty-four-year-old male, but many teens and preteens also enjoy this type of gaming.[3]

MMOGs are typically fantasy-based, with two of the biggest titles among hard-core gamers being *World of Warcraft* and *Everquest*. In fact, the fantasy-based category accounts for 89 percent of the market share among online games. Sci-fi and superhero games are next in popularity. Many of the Web sites for these games involve a free trial to entice the gamers to play. Once they're hooked, a small subscription fee is charged each month. While the investment to play is usually quite nominal, the MMOG category generates an estimated $350 *billion* in revenue each year.[4]

VIRTUAL LIFE MEETS REALITY

One of the most popular MMOGs falls into the generic category known as role-playing games (RPGs). These are where players assume the role of a character they've created. Though many RPGs involve fighting otherworldly creatures such as orcs, goblins, and elves, in recent years the category has branched out into territory that looks more like real life. This is particularly true with massively multiplayer online RPGs, known as—you guessed it—MMORPGs. Following in the footsteps of the popular computer game *The Sims*, these titles allow players to live parallel lives online, complete with dating, marriage, jobs, etc. While this concept may seem strange to some parents, what's sure to surprise most is the extent to which these games blur fantasy and reality.

The makers of online game *Entropia Universe*, for example, have found a way for players to actually make real money playing video games. Frame of reference: In many online games, players compete for the tools they need to continue on their quests. Often these tools include weaponry, an increase in power, or additional "lives" to extend their playing time. But just like in reality, money is sometimes required to complete a transaction in a game. Up until recently, any financial gain was purely virtual.

NOT ANYMORE.

In 2006, Entropia Universe's makers, a Swedish software company named MindArk, created an actual ATM card by which any of the game's 500,000 registered players from across the world could use a real-life ATM to convert earned virtual points into legitimate cash. By the game's predetermined exchange rate, ten "Project Entropia dollars," or PED, are worth U.S. $1. While that may mean little to you, consider this: In 2005, $165 million passed through the game, and MindArk expected that number to double in 2006.[5]

HOW MUCH IS TOO MUCH?

Chances are that even if your own kids *are* into online gaming, they probably haven't gone so far as to raid Mom's purse or Dad's wallet to pay for "virtual property." Neither are they likely anytime soon to elope with the "owner" of their online character's girlfriend. At the same time, how many times have you seen them forsake real-life chores, activities, schoolwork, or even relationships all for "just one more hour" in their virtual world?

At the core of these online video games is the fact that, like most everything else online, they rarely have a definitive ending. Whereas you can win, lose, or simply "finish" single-player games, most online games focus on characters and their interactive environment that often mirror real life. Portable gaming devices help to further that reality, making it possible for truly dedicated (or should that be addicted?) gamers to keep on playing wherever they go.

Olivia and Kurt Bruner learned firsthand about this from their son, Kyle. What started out as a simple purchase of a Nintendo system when Kyle was in elementary school turned into an obsession. By the time he was a teenager, the Bruners' son was addicted to video games.

In their book *Playstation Nation*, the Bruners share openly and honestly about the addictive nature of video games. While relaying the story of how their son became hooked, they identify seven driving forces behind video game addiction, and why young boys in particular seem so prone to becoming gaming addicts. These addictive forces are:

- beating the game
- competition
- mastery
- exploration
- the high score
- story-driven role play
- relationships

In addition to these seven, the Bruners mention how peer pressure plays a big factor in keeping players coming back to the video game world: "Many video and Internet games are designed to create an odd type of peer pressure in which players rely upon each other for support. Gamers also play for long periods of time to improve their character's skill and attributes in order to stay on par with others. If one does not advance from one level to the next quickly enough, he or she falls behind the pack, risking getting kicked out of the unit."[6]

CHILDREN SEE, CHILDREN DO

If our goal as parents is to *Internet Protect Our Kids*, we must remember that it is *our* example that will have the greatest impact on them. This holds true for video games just as much as it does for the language we use or the attitudes we bear. According to a recent poll conducted by America Online and the Associated Press, 40 percent of American *adults* play video games on a regular basis. More than half said they play on a video console, while 45 percent also game online. In addition, 20 percent of adults feel their gaming has enabled them to form new friendships or relationships with fellow gamers they had never known before.[7]

Is it any wonder, then, how those adults' kids feel about video games?

Father-of-four Cameron Wright considers himself a "hardcore gamer." Maybe that's because one of the investment manager's dearest personal investments is his gaming center. At forty-four years old, Wright shrugs off the notion that video games are just kids' play. Last year, he spent more than $4,500 on his "hobby," most of that on upgrades to two of the four personal computers he has in his home. Wright says he typically spends about two hours a week gaming, though he admits that his favorite games—those in the military-strategy genre—eat up much more time, partly because he's playing online with friends. "Once you start . . . you're looking at four to five hours a night."[8]

Fortunately, Wright doesn't seem to lose track of his primary role as a dad. Instead, he uses video games as a chance for family fun time. "We find ourselves sitting down and passing [the controller] around from one person to another doing round-robin tournaments," Wright says. "The kids just eat that up. The big competition is who gets through that level first."

If Your Kids Are Already Gamers

If your children show signs of being addicted to an online game, have them remove themselves from the game immediately. Then, sit down with them and look at the games they want to play online. Learn as much as you can about each game before passing judgment, and be sure to get your children involved in the research process. Kids are more likely to support what they help to create, so their involvement in arriving at the decision as to whether or not they should play an online game will go a long way toward their abiding by that final call.

Like most forms of entertainment, video gaming isn't inherently bad in moderation. And whereas some dads spend thousands a year on cars, golf clubs, and "big-boy toys," Wright's passion just happens to be gaming. The key, however, is making sure that, as parents, our actions are sending the right message. It's an old cliché, but kids learn more from what is *caught* than what is *taught*.

If you or your spouse enjoys video games to the point that it interrupts family life, guess who's picking up on that the most? Likewise, if you (either of you) spend more time playing games

---

Are We Having Fun Yet?
Take a "family physical" and see how you're doing in the fun and recreation department. If the only things you're doing for fun are staying at home and watching movies or playing games online, make the commitment to incorporate an "electronics-free" fun time each week. Go for a walk or a bike ride as a family. Play a board game together—and not online! Enjoy each other's company, and include some fun food while you're at it. Watch what happens when everyone makes enough room in their busy schedule for real connection to take place!

---

online than with the family, your actions are telling your kids that this is an acceptable standard. On a larger scale, if you consume media over the Internet, you're endorsing this practice for your children as well. And if the Internet is your main source of entertainment, why shouldn't it be the place where your children can be entertained as well?

Can you see how important it is for you to model a healthy perspective of video gaming—both online and offline—for your kids? Remember, as a parent, *you* set the standard not just with lip service, but with your everyday actions.

LET KIDS BE KIDS

With all the concerns about the safety of online relationships and the addictive nature of video games, we parents can easily make the mistake of dismissing all video games as inherently evil. In fact, that is simply not the case. We must also remember that there are many reasons why children are drawn to video games, but at the heart of their desire is the fact that they love and need to *play!* Playtime is a time for recreation, for literally *re-creating the soul.* Preteens and especially teens require this playtime for dozens of reasons. Sure, too much fun can be unhealthy and lead to an imbalanced life. But make no mistake, kids need to have fun regularly in their lives, and it is possible for that fun to include a moderated quantity of video gaming.

In his book *The 10 Building Blocks for a Happy Family*, parenting and family expert Dr. Jim Burns writes about the importance of family playtime. "We know instinctively that play produces family togetherness and support," he says. "We know that when we play together, we have a deeper sense of belonging and community in the family. . . . Humor heals broken families."[9] Kids need a place to play and laugh, and many are finding their fun either online or through video games—or both. While there's nothing inherently wrong with this, it's up to us as their parents to show them how to use the Internet responsibly for recreation. And make sure their online fun is balanced with some good old-fashioned playtime *outdoors* as well.

⇚

Internet Protect Your Kids Against Harmful Entertainment Choices by:

1. Researching popular movies, television shows, music, and video games to see what they're really about rather than relying upon a rating system.
2. Organizing a "Family Media Night" in your home so you can compare notes with other parents on the entertainment media your kids want to watch, listen to, and play.
3. Monitoring the content in "free" online offers to make

sure it's appropriate for your children before allowing them to download it.

4. Restricting access to massively multiplayer online games (MMOGs) until you and your son or daughter have thoroughly "done your homework" to see if the game in question is appropriate for playing.

5. Scheduling a regular time of family fun each week that does not involve the use of any form of electronic media, such as a movie or video game.

Chapter 10

All They Need to Know: Why the Internet Is Kids' Primary Source for Information

This is so lame. I can't believe this!"

Seventeen-year-old Austin slammed the door as he got into the car. His best friend, Randy, was riding shotgun, but based on Austin's attitude at that moment, he was wondering if he might be better off walking home from school instead.

"Chill, dude. Why are you so uptight?"

"Because my civics teacher is a moron," Austin fumed. "I totally had an A in his class until he gave me a zero on my current events assignment."

"What happened?" Randy asked. "Didn't you turn it in on time?"

"Yeah!" Austin snapped. "But he didn't accept *any* of the articles I wrote about because they didn't come out of a stupid newspaper. How lame is *that*?!"

A New Information Highway

Austin's frustration is understandable. Some members of older generations have a hard time legitimizing information unless it's "in print." While that phrase is loosely applied—TV and radio news broadcasts have always been considered authentic—there's a sense that the Internet is nothing but a bunch of people posting unverified information and personal opinions. In their minds, *real* news isn't found online, and therefore the Web as a whole can't be taken seriously.

With all due respect to those people, the truth is that the Internet is just as authentic as every other new medium that's emerged in the past 100 years. It is not only changing and shaping the way news is delivered today, it's leading the way. Television networks, newspapers, radio stations, movie studios . . . they've all rushed to establish a significant Web presence with the latest online technology. And the result is that news has become an up-to-the-second process available in unprecedented amounts to anyone and everyone.

Is it any surprise, then, that Austin's generation is far more inclined to get news headlines online than from a newspaper? The Internet has become the primary *information* source for kids. And that means *all* of the information they need, not just news headlines. Whether they're looking for sports scores, weather conditions, celebrity gossip, or the latest information on their finances, the MySpace Generation looks to the Internet first to get the job done. Wireless or "WiFi" connections make it possible to stay connected even when they're not at home or at school. Research projects that once required hours in the library buried under mountains of *Encyclopedia Brittanica* volumes are now completed from the comfort of home or a dorm room with the help of a vast assortment of online resources, all of which are just a click away.

FROM ENCYCLOPEDIA TO WIKIPEDIA

Jimmy Wales is at the forefront of this online revolution. He's the founder of Wikipedia.com, perhaps the world's first online encyclopedia to ever serve the international market. Launched in 2001, Wikipedia is a collection of almost four *million* articles in an impressive 250 languages (more than one and a half million entries are in English) cobbled together by an assortment of contributors. In other words, it's a communal, open-ended encyclopedia. A "wiki" is a software program that allows virtually anyone to add to, edit, or even delete an entry based upon his or her knowledge of the topic. Whereas a collection like the *Encyclopedia Brittanica* is compiled by a consortium of scholars, Wikipedia is open to anyone who has knowledge about a topic, regardless of their level of expertise.

This can obviously create some factual problems, as Wikipedia has been aware of since it inception. For example, several biographical entries on living people recently proved to be erroneous, including one red herring naming a well-known journalist as a suspect in the assassinations of both President John F. Kennedy and his brother.[1] However, Wikipedia has tried to keep a high standard by monitoring entries and requiring verification for information. (Users can report "false" information.) In addition, a new editing tool has been introduced that makes it easier to both amend and verify existing Wikipedia entries.

Nevertheless, the minor snags aren't making a difference among kids and young adults, who are flocking to the site. In fact, eighteen- to twenty-four-year-olds are twice as likely to use Wikipedia for encyclopedic information than any other resource.[2] They like the flexibility the "wiki" affords them and the fact that they can become active participants in defining the terms they're looking up.

Take, for example, a high school student who is doing a project on a piece of literature by Shakespeare. If she used Wikipedia to research her own paper, it's wouldn't be out of the ordinary for her to then turn around and add her own project to the reference list of that same entry on Shakespeare's writing. Because it makes history more interactive, this aspect of Wikipedia has tremendous appeal to the experiential-based Generation @.

BLOG A THOUGHT

The success of Wikipedia among the under-twenty-five crowd isn't surprising, given the importance these kids and young adults

> **When Blogging Turns Offensive**
> If you discover that your child is blogging in an offensive manner, take action immediately. Profanity-laden online tirades are a cry for help, so don't just chalk them up as a reaction to peer pressure. Also, if your child is part of an online group or forum centering on deviant or dangerous behavior, suspend all Internet privileges until you have time to do a more thorough investigation of how he got involved in the first place.

place on self-expression. Yet while the encyclopedic site allows for only so much creative freedom given its fact-based nature, blogging provides a boundaryless canvas. Whether on their own Web sites or the personal profile pages of social networking sites, kids are soaking up the opportunity to share their inner thoughts and feelings with anyone willing to read. For example, the following poem was posted on a blog of a MySpace user:

> *I love you is eight letters*
> *so is bull——*
> *you lied right to my face*
> *when you said we would stay together*
> *but now you're gone*
> *and I lost the key to my own heart*
> *you can take your lies*
> *and your love*
> *give them to someone new*
> *just don't break her heart*
> *like you broke mine . . .*[3]

It doesn't take a psychologist to see these deeply personal thoughts were penned by someone in pain—a teenager, to be exact. She's certainly not the first teen to write out her feelings. In fact, she's simply one of the millions of kids who now choose blogging as their primary, if not *only*, form of processing what's on their minds and in their hearts. To no one's surprise, girls ages fifteen to seventeen are the most common bloggers among the younger age group. One recent study indicated that as many as 25 percent of girls in this age group who go online have personal blogs and update them at least once a week.[4]

Sometimes bloggers will wax poetic, other times philosophical or political. But when kids blog, their topics typically center on subjects such as love, pain, betrayal, and longing. One teenage girl recently posted this poem, perhaps as a way of dealing with the infidelity that may have hit her own home:

A drink,
a thought,
a kiss,
he leads the faceless woman to their unforsaken fate.

Read Without Reacting

More often than not, kids use their blogs as a place to vent. This means every now and then they might choose to blog right after a heated argument with someone they really love and respect—someone like you.

If you read something hurtful in your child's blog, do everything you can to keep your composure. Walt Mueller of the Center for Parent/Youth Understanding says it best: "Read without reacting!"[5] Obviously, that's much easier said than done. But for starters, remind yourself that your children need an outlet to express their thoughts and frustrations—and it's good that they're doing that rather than keeping it pent up inside. The problem here is that rather than talk it out with someone else, they're posting their frustrations publicly.

Remember, kids tend to think they're invisible and invincible online. So if you come across something in your child's blog that's offensive or even hurtful toward you, your family, or your faith, do everything in your power to keep your composure, but be sure to use those entries as "discussion starters" with your child at a later date.

His, to a broken household and an unfaithful marriage,
and hers,
to confusion and false love.
He arrives home, drunk, no thoughts,
a kiss, to his faithful wife, and the tragedy continues . . .[6]

It's no secret that many kids today are hurting. They're feeling the effects of trying to regain lost love in a broken home. They're longing for a sense of security from loved ones who can't or won't provide it. Obviously, not every kid these days is dealing with pain this great, but for those who are, the Internet is providing them with a place to vent their frustrations. And when they go online, they can usually find a sympathetic friend to hear them out.

Reading beyond the blogs, it becomes evident that there's a reason for the ambivalence that's expressed by so many teens and preteens online. In many ways, they're hoping to connect with someone else who will understand. At the same time, they harbor a deep hope that blogging will be the way they can get their feelings off their chest without the embarrassment of too many people knowing their deepest, darkest secrets—spelling and grammar errors notwithstanding.

This is my Emo Poem . . . becuz I was bored in all my class-
es so I wrote this and yes, sometimes this is [truly] how I feel . . .
I am very proud of this.

When the darkness fades, a fire burns inside, a fire I cannot
prevent. It burns so excessively I find myself crippled with fear.
A fear I don't know how to contain. There are shadows cast upon
the heavy walls, they enfold me, containing my screams. There is
no one to confide [in], I sit here wallowing in my own self-pity.
My loneliness is my suicide, not a knife that cuts, but my own
stabbing heart beat. I lay my head down to rest, with cuts so deep,
I know nothing of my future, yet I am driven by my suffering to
a new day.[7]

FOR THE GOOD

Not all blogs are filled with pain and heartache. Some can be insightful and even inspiring:

I just got home from a beautiful weekend and I have some thoughts. All the gazing into the sunsets/sunrises made me realize that I have such a good life. I don't know it's just like everyone talks about how they have this and that to do and how much their life is sucking right now but really, think about it. We live in an amazing area where there isn't a lot of violence and we're pret-

---

Blogging 101

If the concept of blogging is new to you, you'll want to find a blog to read and see for yourself how they work. Of course, with literally millions of blogs on the Internet, you may not know where to start. HomeWord's resident blogging expert is Hugh Hewitt, so we'd recommend visiting his Web site at www.hughhewitt.com. It features a fairly comprehensive listing of the most credible blogs online, so you should be able to find something you deem worth reading.

Establishing a blog is fairly simple: You set up a blog address on the Internet, post your thoughts on a particular topic, and then "push" those thoughts to fellow bloggers to let them know you're out there. Once they read your comments and respond, another blog is born!

---

ty wealthy. But it's more than that. I know that I have the best friends anyone could ever ask for, I have a blast ALL the time . . . well most of the time. I have an amazing family and I'm pretty much taken care of. And beyond THAT I have a strong faith with God that made those moments in the sun this weekend even more appreciated. Now, just close your eyes, think of some place you absolutely love and wander . . . know once you open your eyes, just soak your life in kid, cause it's freaking awesome!!!![8]

For the most part, blogging can be a healthy outlet for teens and preteens when used in an appropriate manner. According to a research presented at the 2006 American Association for the

Advancement of Science conference, young people now have as many opportunities, if not more, to practice leadership and develop social skills online as they did before the Internet was around.[9] And blogging is a big part of that.

Unlike instant messaging, which carries on more like a conversation, bloggers often tap into a more creative side of their personalities. And, as the parent of a teen or preteen, you may be pleasantly surprised at what your son or daughter might choose to blog about.

THE "SCANDAL" THAT WASN'T

Blogs can be both entertaining and educational. Yet during the 2004 Presidential election, they took on a more serious tone— one that ultimately impacted both public perception of blogs and the entire practice of news reporting.

You undoubtedly remember the situation: That summer, incumbent Republican President George W. Bush was battling popular Democratic Party candidate John Kerry in an election that would generate the greatest voter turnout in our nation's history. A couple of months before Election Day, CBS News filed

---

Take the "New Media" Challenge

There's a good possibility that your kids will be blogging about current events they've only read about online or from another blog. So why not become a student of the culture and give up your newspaper for a week? Turn off the television while you're at it, and get your news of the world exclusively from the Internet. There are many credible services from which to choose—MSNBC.com and FoxNews.com among the more reliable. See how using only online reporting for one week affects the way you look at world events. Remember that doing so will help you discover a window into the soul of your under-twenty-five child in the process. And if you're really feeling adventuresome, why not consider starting a family blog so that you and your kids can have a place to share personal news with friends and extended family as well!

---

a report about a leak of some highly sensitive "official" documents indicating that President Bush had received "preferential treatment" while serving in the National Guard during the Vietnam War.[10]

A generation or two ago, such reporting might have led to a federal investigation, possibly along the lines of the scandal surrounding the break-in at the Watergate Hotel in 1972. This being the twenty-first century, however, the common public didn't just take CBS' claims at face value, but instead went about their business of searching out the truth—and then posting it on blogs. In fact, the blogging community almost immediately called CBS News on the carpet for "leaking" a report that turned out to be a non-story.

That a major television network could act so capriciously was a concern to many. Yet what really turned heads was not only the dizzying speed with which the blogging community uncovered the truth, but also the fact that blogs were now being recognized as credible sources of news and information. This may have been a shock to anyone over the age of twenty-five, but to kids and young adults it was merely confirmation of what they already knew: Blogs were in; the "dinosaur media" was out.

On the surface, this seemed to be the kind of political scandal that American adults have grown weary of hearing about. Once the dust had settled, the facts of the case were revealed, the accused vindicated, and an apology offered by CBS News (along with a few firings and one tainted career of Dan Rather). Possibly more important that all of this, however, was that the Internet was now officially seen as a reliable vehicle for the truth.

HERE TODAY, GONE TOMORROW

This day has been coming for several years. Newspaper and magazine readership has been on the decline for decades. Younger, hipper styles of reporting and "youth-focused" features haven't

---

Blogging and Internet Safety

If your kids are already blogging, it's essential that you have access to any and all blogs they're currently contributing to and/or running. For children who only blog on their MySpace profile, gaining this access will be a relatively simple task. If your kids are more involved in the blogging process, however, you may need to invest a weekend and sit down with them to find out every place they like to blog. Either way, get ready to discover some fascinating new things about your children! Be prepared for a potential struggle with them over the content of their blogging, especially if they use it to vent about sensitive personal (and sometimes family-related) information. Yet remember that you're the adult here: Be compassionate and understanding, but also be the parent.

---

been able to save them. Traditional print media is on life support and losing breath simply because the younger generation isn't interested in reading something that's so "out of date" the minute it goes to press. Case in point: *Teen People* and *Elle Girl* were two of the more popular magazines targeting girls ages ten to seventeen, and only years prior had been flourishing with subscription numbers. But in the summer of 2006 both ceased producing a printed publication. Content for each publication is now available exclusively online.

This is Generation @ we're talking about here. They're driven by instant access, on-demand, and online twenty-four-seven. They're also amoral. This doesn't make them bad people; rather, they simply view the world as something that is defined by *their* terms. Since they believe that there are no moral absolutes, who is to say what is "newsworthy" except them?

That worldview has transformed the entire arena of information gathering, particularly online. Those in Generation @ like their info delivered anytime and all the time, so they're particularly fond of online news reports and updates. But they're also consumed, if not completely obsessed, with what's happening in *their* lives. Enter blogging, which gives kids the opportunity to have both factual news and room to rant emotionally all in the same space. And *where* do those rants take place most often, you ask? Social networking sites, of course!

MORPHING INTO A MODERN-DAY BLOG

When Xanga.com was first created, its founders designed it to be a place for aspiring writers to showcase their work. Little did they realize that their site would soon be hijacked by millions of teenagers who turned it into a "kid blog" that soon mushroomed to thirty million users.

The Xanga creators also quickly discovered another thing: Words don't always have the same impact on this demographic as they might on an older generation. Generation @ is *visually* driven, so a site that's all about words—and only words—could prove to be an "it" site for a while, but eventually younger users would want more than just text-based blogs with a few pictures thrown in for appearance's sake. They'd want streaming video and music—lots of music. And why just blog when you can create a myriad of other features as part of your very own personal Web page?

It's no coincidence that social networking sites like MySpace, Facebook, Friendster, and (an ever-changing) Xanga were beginning to establish a foothold in the marketplace of ideas around the same time that CBS was taken to the proverbial woodshed by the blogging community. By the summer of 2004, millions of kids and young adults were enjoying their own virtual community on sites like these. That some of their fellow bloggers were able to garner the attention of the mainstream media was merely an added bonus.

"The Medium Is the Message"

We have entered an era in which technology is no longer merely a means to an end. In many cases, it has become the end itself. When scholar and media guru Marshall McLuhan said that "the medium is the message," it's possible he didn't anticipate the advent of Internet blogging and social networking sites.[11] But for kids and young adults under the age of twenty-five, the medium is both the message *and* the messenger. And no doubt, Generation @ will continue to utilize online technology as its primary source of receiving and sending information—at least until the next cultural revolution comes along.

Internet Protect Your Kids When They Blog by:

1. Suspending all Internet privileges immediately if you discover they are part of an online group or forum centering on deviant or dangerous behavior.
2. "Reading without reacting" when you come across something they have blogged about that is hurtful to you, your family, or your faith.
3. Familiarizing yourself with blogging by finding a blog you will read regularly, even if that means starting your own!
4. Abandoning your newspaper and television news reports for one week, and replacing them with only online reports instead. This will give you a better feel for the way your child is keeping up with current events.
5. Gaining access to any and all blogs they currently contribute to and/or host.

Chapter 11

IT'S *YOUR* WORLD:
WHY KIDS LOVE SOCIAL
NETWORKING SITES

U p to this point, we've looked at some of the surface reasons why our kids want to socialize on the Internet. We've mentioned the community aspect of sites such as MySpace, and the sense of belonging that these places provide kids. Gone are the days of kowtowing to the popular kids at school just to find a group of friends. Now teens and preteens can simply create a profile on MySpace and literally have millions of potential friends to choose from—and millions more who might just choose them as well. In other words, social networking sites offer instant acceptance; if you can't find it in one chat room, just move on to the next one.

We've also talked about the self-expression element and how important that is to Generation @. Whether through creating a MySpace page, blogging, or simply I Ming, the online arena provides an endless landscape for these kids to create and express whatever they want. And, of course, we've covered the connection aspect, how kids have the ability to pick and choose whom they connect with based exclusively on similar interests—without having to worry about all the differences and "extras."

If we truly want to *Internet Protect Our Kids,* however, we'll

---

Internet Basics for Younger Children

As your younger kids begin to venture into the world of social networking, they may feel a negative peer pressure to share their online information with everyone online. Teach your kids that it is perfectly acceptable to not respond to every e-mail they receive. If they're new to the concept of spamming, they'll soon discover how much e-mail is actually junk. And if your kids have instant messaging privileges, it won't take long before they learn that a real friend will never pass along IM account information without their prior consent. They'll learn that lesson the moment an unsolicited IM comes their way!

---

need to go beyond these appealing aspects about the Web and instead look to the root cause of why they're so invested in this virtual world. Why do our kids feel that the Internet can meet so many of their felt needs? Because whether we realize it or not, that's exactly how most of them view their online experience. To them, the Internet is the perfect vehicle for communication, recreation, information, and self-expression—all in one. It's also the one place most kids feel they can completely control.

I'M IN CONTROL

It's also the one place most kids feel they can completely control. What insecure, developing child *doesn't* want to be able to "call the shots" in her life? Social networking Web sites give her that opportunity—or at least that's how it *feels* to her. And remember, to the under-twenty-five set, *experience* is truth, knowledge, power, and reality. If a child only has positive experiences of creating her own environment online, she'll easily assume that such will *always* be the case. But parents know there's not a Web filter around that can teach your child the common-sense realities of the world. Only *you* can do that, Mom and Dad!

Unfortunately, the Internet only helps further the "fantasy reality" so many kids develop. It offers the one place where kids can pick whatever age they want to be and take on that persona online. As a result, they gain a sense of authority and power. Keep in mind, this is the generation that was taught how to use a condom in the second grade and then told that twenty-five years of age was "too young" to rush into an important decision such as whether or not to marry or which career to choose. In other words, most of these kids already have a dichotomous moral sense to guide them; the Web simply muddles this by offering fantasy and acceptance on all sides.

On the Internet, younger kids can "age up" without having to grow up, while older ones can stay young in an effort to work through some of their fears of facing their twenties and thirties. If you have younger kids, that means you'll likely need to work with them to resist their natural tendency to want to grow up too soon. And if you have older kids you're responsible for, you'll want to treat each situation on a case-by-case basis.

Internet Usage Rules for Older Kids

Just because you have kids who are eighteen or older doesn't mean you no longer have parental authority over their computer use. College students who still live at home should be under the authority of their parents' rules. The same holds true if your kids are away at college but you are paying their way there. "House rules" don't end the moment your son or daughter earns a high school diploma or turns eighteen.

CONTROL AT YOUR FINGERTIPS

One of the biggest driving forces behind this age shift and power play is the social networking site. SNSes allow kids to piece together a completely alternative life than their real one. They can choose different friends than they normally would, act differently, use different language . . . and on and on. In fact, on a personal level, the social networking phenomenon could one day be looked at as the most revolutionary development to come out of the Information Age.

Be the Change

Help your kids to see themselves as content creators as well as Internet users. Doing so will enable them to realize the role they can play in making social networking sites safer and healthier for all users. There is no neutral ground online. Kids who want to communicate through IMing, text messaging, SNSes are either part of the problem or part of the solution. Do all you can to help your children become problem-solvers.

Simply put, it's all about control. SNS users love the influence they can exert on a certain sphere of other users. And the scope of that sphere is completely up to them. Yet SNS sites are certainly not the only ones on the Internet creating this artificial sense of absolute control. Among thousands, two companies stand out in recent years for their influence on making the buck stop not with big-name franchises, but with the individual user.

In the fall of 1995, a computer programmer named Pierre Omidyar developed Auctionweb, an online auction site. The first item he ever sold was a broken laser pointer. Purchase price: $13.83. Omidyar was amazed that someone would actually want his broken device, so he e-mailed the person who placed the winning bid to find out if he realized what he had just purchased. The man responded that he did, and it was okay because he collected broken laser pointers. At that moment, Omidyar knew he was onto something. So he hired a small staff and began to grow his business.

You probably know the rest of the story. A consulting firm that Omidyar used called Echo Bay Technology Group was giving up its Web site. Omidyar wanted it for his own business and tried to register for the domain name of EchoBay.com, but another group had already snatched it up. As a result, he shortened the domain name to eBay.com, and the world of online retail transactions has never been the same.[1]

INFORMATION ORGANIZATION

A couple of months after Pierre Omidyar founded what became the prototype for online retailing, a couple of Ph.D. candidates at Stanford University were about to take search engines into an entirely different dimension.

In January 1996, Larry Page and Sergey Brin figured that the best search engine would be one that connected the myriad of smaller, less-efficient search engines that were popping up all over the Internet. Because the system checked the number of links between sites to gauge the importance of searching any given site in particular, the pair originally called their service "BackRub." Today, however, it's known as Google, and has become the universal definitive model for search engines.[2]

eBay created a new platform for how retail transactions were handled online. In much the same way, Google created a new standard for the organization of information. Mozilla's Firefox program is also doing the same thing with increasing popularity because of its reputation for basing its site rankings on actual usage regardless of whether or not a domain has been registered

---

Finding an Online Club

Become a student of the culture your kids are living in by browsing through the "Clubs" or "Forums" section of MySpace with your son or daughter. You'll find literally tens of thousands of different clubs, most of which are free to join once users have an account with MySpace. If your child doesn't find a club he is interested in (or that you approve of), he can create a new one more to his liking.

Some of the existing clubs have only a few members, others number in the tens of thousands. There are more than 77,000 groups categorized as "religious" on MySpace; two of the largest are "Hardcore Christians Living Hardcore," with around 67,000 members, and "The Christian Teens of MySpace," with a membership of more than 63,000.[3] Most of the clubs are open to the public of MySpace account holders, but a good number of them are private, meaning you must be invited to join.

Bring a *Real* Perspective

The Internet is not going away. Online social networking is here to stay. And your kids are learning how to cope with the stresses of modern life and the insecurities of adolescence by finding instant acceptance online with a peer group they feel like they can trust, along with a sense of control over their virtual world. Your job as a parent is to help them distinguish between fact and fantasy. It is impossible to have an authentic relationship and real connection with a "cyber-penpal" they've only swapped IMs with online. Be the parent. Encourage your kids to make real friends in real life and use the Internet to only enhance those relationships, not establish them.

---

with them. Each of these innovative companies has revolutionized how we "grab" material, in these cases, retail transactions and information. Yet what makes MySpace and other social networking sites so influential is that they connect people to people, not just users to information or products.

A WORLD UNTO ITSELF

The eBay and Google models rely on the marketplace to provide them with the resources they provide for their consumers. The MySpace model, on the other hand, is completely self-sufficient.

Let that fact ruminate around in your brain for just a moment. When your child goes on MySpace, he's not just a "consumer" of what the site has to offer; he's creating his own material and exchanging it in this online marketplace of ideas.

In essence, your child becomes a *commodity* on MySpace. His likes, dislikes, attitudes, hobbies, and friends all become part of the "economy" he's supporting. He has "currency" to spend—and he'll be happy to spend it all right! But this phenomenon affects more than just our kids individually.

Think of the impact MySpace is already having on the world of media and entertainment distribution. As we mentioned in a previous chapter, new projects (e.g., music CDs, movies, video games) used to be sold via cleverly designed marketing campaigns to get kids to buy into whatever concept that project embodied. That, in turn led to the purchase of the movie ticket, CD, or game—and all the cross-promotional product that went with it. On social networking sites, however, the *consumers* are also the *producers* of said concept. *They're* the ones calling the shots, not multimillion-dollar companies. This presents an unforeseen dilemma for parents regarding the way we can control the media content to which our kids might be exposed.

Under the old media model, the more successful businesses were usually afforded the choice locations in town to sell their wares. And remember the axiom that every seller swore by: "The three keys to success in retailing are *location, location, location!*" At the same time, the old media model of retailing also banished undesirable goods and services to locations that were not readily accessible, making them easier to avoid. For example, pornographic movies and magazines were generally sold through the mail or in so-called "adult bookstores" that were usually in lousy parts of town. It wasn't all that difficult for parents to keep their kids away from these places because it took a true act of will and determination for a kid to actually go to one of them, let alone buy anything from them.

EVERYTHING IS ACCESSIBLE
The new model for media production and consumption is the exact opposite. No longer are we ruled by "pull" or "grab" distribution. "Push" is the order of the day, with under-twenty-fivers not only pushing media that they create on their own, but they're also pushing the work of their friends as well. All the more reason for you as a parent to get involved and *stay involved* with what your kids are doing online.

When they tell you that they just keep a few pictures of their friends in their Photobucket account (an online "photo album" site), ask to see those pictures. While it may create an awkward tension between you and your child for a season, you're better off having asked and discovered there's nothing there than to find out after the fact that your daughter took some topless photos of herself and posted them on her MySpace profile.

Kids have a tendency to think that they have complete control over what they say and do over the Internet. They can create a sense of connection with their online friends that, in essence, amounts to little more than false intimacy and false security. What they don't realize is how badly they need your guidance as a parent to keep them from acting foolishly and irresponsibly online. They may not thank you right away for your involvement—in fact, they may not show their appreciation for another twenty-five years—but deep down, they'll be grateful. And the security you provide could lead your children to create the next eBay, Google, or MySpace. And, when they do, you can count on the fact that they'll hold a seat on the board of directors for *you*!

Internet Protect Your Kids from a False Sense of Online Control by:

1. Reminding them often that it's perfectly acceptable to not respond to every e-mail or Instant Message they receive.
2. Consistently enforcing the "house rules" for Internet use even after they graduate from high school or turn eighteen.
3. Encouraging them to be online problem-solvers and content creators, not just consumers.
4. Becoming a student of their culture by browsing through the "Clubs" or "Forums" section of MySpace with your son or daughter.
5. Helping them distinguish between fact and fantasy, and preventing them from substituting online relationships for real-life ones.

Chapter 12

INTERNET SAFETY FOR YOUR KIDS: PRAYERFUL, PURPOSEFUL, PREPARED, AND PROACTIVE

Michelle and her husband, Dave, were used to getting compliments on how well-behaved their daughters were. Seventeen-year-old Jessie and fourteen-year-old Vanessa were excellent students who made wise choices when it came to friends and building their faith.

Because they both attended the same high school and had many similar interests, Jessie and Vanessa hung out together with many of the same kids. Jessie was the unofficial big sister of the bunch, so she wound up driving to a lot of the social events both girls attended—movies, school dances, church activities, and the like. Neither Michelle nor Dave had reason to worry when the girls were out with their friends because they always received a check-in call from one of their daughters. It was usually Vanessa who handled the phone duties, and her responsibility impressed her parents. Because of this, she was often rewarded with a later curfew on the nights she was out with her older sister.

When Jessie graduated from high school and went off to

college, Vanessa continued hanging out with the group that remained from her high school. She was fifteen now and still a very responsible kid. On her first night out with the remainder of "the gang," though, Dave and Michelle were a bit surprised when they didn't get a check-in call. They began to worry as Vanessa's curfew time of 10:30 p.m. came and went, and there was still no word from their younger daughter. By the time she finally strode through the door, it was just before 11:15—a full quarter-hour before her sister's old curfew time, but well past her own.

Michelle was furious. "Vanessa! Do you have *any* idea what time it is?"

"Yeah, Mom. It's 11:15."

"You're *late*!"

"*Late*? I thought I didn't have to be home till 11:30."

"Well, that was when you were with your sister. *Her* curfew was 11:30."

At that moment, Dave spoke up. "I have to admit I'm a bit surprised at your behavior, Vanessa. Not only did you miss your curfew time, but you didn't check in once the whole evening."

"Oh, sorry, Dad. I guess I just forgot to call."

"*Forgot to call*? But Vanessa, you were the one who *always* called to check in when you were out with your sister. How could you just all of a sudden *forget* to call us?"

Vanessa looked a bit surprised that both of her parents seemed so upset with her. She genuinely thought that her curfew had also been 11:30, so she was actually under the impression that she had gotten home early. And as for the phone call, there was a perfectly good reason why she didn't check in with her parents, at least as far as she was concerned.

"I didn't just *all of a sudden* forget to call you, Daddy. I *never* thought about stuff like that when I was hanging out with Jessie. She always hated having to drive me everywhere, so when it was time to check in, she would throw me her cell and say, 'Hey, *I* have to drive you everywhere, so *you* have to check in with Mom and Dad. So call them.' And I would."

Dave and Michelle were speechless. In the span of a little over three minutes one evening, they found out the hard way that *everything* they thought they understood about how their daughters behaved when they weren't around their Mom and Dad had just gone right out the window.

SHOCK TO THE SYSTEM

Think back to the way you felt when you first found out that your kids were spending so much time online. These nice, innocent, well-behaved children you were so proud of seemed to turn into these "other people" when you discovered what they were putting in their MySpace profiles. They had an entirely different set of friends than the ones you knew. Could they be trusted? Could you ever trust your own kids again after finding out about their "other" lives? The good news is, you *can* . . . but it's going to take a bit of work to rebuild that trust.

Noted author and blogging expert Hugh Hewitt likens a lack of parental supervision of kids online to "handing a sixteen-year old a bottle of Scotch and the car keys *before* she's ever had a driving lesson."[1] You wouldn't willingly allow your child to roam free and unsupervised in a lawless country if he only knew a little bit of the language. So why let him wander around on the Internet with no parental guidance or guidelines?

Keep in mind, the Internet is completely neutral when it comes to morals and values. It only contains the content created for it and the values that are a part of that content. The law isn't always going to protect your kids from the images they might see online. Remember, the U.S. Supreme Court generically defined pornography as something we would know when we saw it. Laws protecting minors from exposure to pornographic images are flimsy at best. Many pornographers have been able to successful-ly claim their First Amendment right of free speech as the defense of the obscene content they make available online. Parents can no longer expect the courts to come to their defense, as the judicial silence has proven. So it's up to us, as parents, to instill into our children a sense of decency when it comes to identifying harmful content online.

THE FOUR P'S OF INTERNET SAFETY

Obviously, there is no magic pill or secret formula that will automatically keep your kids safe online. But there are things you can do to help avoid the pitfalls of the Internet—and it starts with the four P's: being *prayerful, purposeful, prepared,* and *proactive.*

1. Be *prayerful.*

There is no earthly way to protect your children without the help of heaven. If you haven't already learned this as a parent, allow us to expose any false security in your own parenting skills—because, as any veteran parent can attest, it's the truth. The best safety precautions you can take pale in comparison to the knowledge and assurance that the hand of God is guiding and protecting your kids. They may occasionally wind up walking down a path that might look like "the valley of the shadow of death" online, but steady doses of prayer cover can minimize the damage, if not avoid it altogether.

Dr. Jim Burns, president of HomeWord Ministries, takes this concept of "prayer cover" a step further. He encourages parents to put together a support system of adults for each of your kids. In addition to Mom and Dad, look for a youth worker or ministry leader who can speak spiritually into the life of your son or daughter, preferably someone who is a bit closer in age to your child. It's also helpful to establish a small prayer team for each kid.

Having this kind of support team in place provides a great opportunity for grandparents, aunts, uncles, and other extended family members to come alongside your children. But it also affords some of the senior members of your church congregation who can grandparent your kids through prayer to help out as well.

2. Be *purposeful*.

It's one thing to *say* you want to keep your kids safe online . . . but don't stop there. Make sure your prayers and actions are *purposeful*.

When Janet's oldest son was getting ready to head to college, she had a revelation:

"I wanted to make sure he remembered the family rules about Internet use while he was away. I had heard so many stories about college students getting involved with drugs and pornography online, and I didn't want him to become a statistic. So I went to print out a copy of the Internet Usage Agreement we had established for the whole family several years ago, and that's when it hit me. We wrote this thing up when Trey was in middle school. The Internet has changed so much since then, and we haven't done *anything* to address those changes."

Give Janet, her husband, and their kids credit for actually *having* an Internet Usage Agreement in the first place. But don't follow their example of simply writing one up and then never looking at it again. The Internet is in a constant state of evolution, so you may need to consider making *monthly* or even *weekly* adjustments to yours. Be *purposeful* in the safeguards you take to protect your kids online.

3. Be *prepared*.

When John and Christy's daughter started middle school, they knew she'd need to go through a period of adjustment to get used to her new surroundings. What they *didn't* count on was their daughter's newfound desire to become the instant messaging champion of the sixth grade.

"John's job promotion came with a transfer, so we wound up

Chat-room Guidelines

No teen or preteen should be allowed to enter an online chat room without prior parental knowledge and consent. If chat-room privileges are granted, access should be limited to chatting only with those known to the child and his or her family. Under no circumstances should chatting be permitted with an acquaintance made only online.

---

moving to a different state one week before Amber started middle school," Christy noted. "Since she didn't have time to make new friends during the summer, we wanted to do all we could to help her get to know her new classmates that first week of school. So we let her establish an IM account so she could chat with some of her new friends online."

A noble gesture on John and Christy's part—but they sorely underestimated how popular Amber would become online. "It seemed like she made more new friends on the first day of middle school than she ever had at her old school," said Christy. "She was always online. Her grades suffered, and so did our family time."

When Amber's buddy list passed the 250-name mark, John and Christy took action. "We knew she was going to be making new friends," John said, "but we had no idea it would be so many. Her buddy list was out of control, so we had to shut down her account and start over."

John and Christy didn't have a problem with Amber having IM privileges. But they felt they needed to do a better job of controlling the number of online friends their daughter had. So they wrote up a usage agreement stating that Amber needed either of her parents' permission to add a buddy to her online address book. Amber could IM for no more than an hour a day, not after 8 p.m., and only when all of her homework for that day was complete.

"Every now and then, Amber will want to add a buddy who

even she doesn't know all that well, and having the IM usage agreement makes it easier for us to say 'no' to those requests," John said. Christy agreed: "Before we had the usage agreement, Amber could have become buddies with a sexual predator who was pretending to be a kid from her school. We were fortunate nothing bad ever happened to her."

4. Be *proactive.*

Many areas of life require preparation before the actual event arrives. Athletic teams practice for hours before entering the arena of competition. Musicians put in countless rehearsal hours before a key performance. When our children are in the womb, we don't just wait around for them to pop out—we spend months preparing a baby room for them, buying cute little baby outfits and nice snuggly blankets. As challenging as we know parenting will be, we at least try to prepare the best we know how for the arrival of our children in this world.

So what makes us think, now that our kids are growing up, we don't have to anticipate dangerous situations, particularly those online? Remember, our kids think they're invincible, so it's up to us as their parents to be proactive in setting up a hedge of protection around them *before* they ever go online. Consider the following advice.

- Caution your kids against setting up an "alternate" profile or IM account that you don't know about. And let them know that if they do, it's going to take a lot of hard work on their part to earn back your trust.
- If your children have never been assigned an online research project before, volunteer to help them come up with one they can propose to their teacher. If they are already receiving online research assignments, suggest to them that you be actively involved in their next project's researching. Doing so will give you both the opportunity

to do some "safe" browsing, and it could also potentially give you the chance to see what can go wrong with a simple misclick of the mouse.

- Visit a video streaming site such as YouTube.com and search out file topics together that seem to line up with your family's values.
- Let your son or daughter select an onscreen icon for your IM account. (Kids love to do this sort of thing, and you probably don't have the time or patience to search one of these out for yourself anyway!)

Internet Protect Your Kids Proactively by:

1. Instilling in them a sense of decency when it comes to identifying harmful content online.
2. Putting together a parental support system that prays regularly for each child represented in the group.
3. Purposefully staying ahead of online trends by updating your Internet Usage Agreement on a regular basis.
4. Continually educating yourself regarding the Internet, while preparing for online situations before they occur.
5. Conducting online research, visiting video sites, and generally surfing the Web with them to acclimate both of you to "safe" sites.

Chapter 13

AN INTERNET FOR GOOD

Fourteen-year-old Scott had been bugging his parents for a MySpace account since he started the eighth grade. Now that he had finally come of age, his parents were considering giving him the opportunity he longed for. But they weren't entirely sure that MySpace was a good place for their son to be, so they went the extra mile and established their own MySpace profiles the same day their son did.

Scott actually thought it was cool that his first MySpace friends were his mom and dad. He also found lots of other kids from his school and his church on MySpace, so his friends list soon grew to more than 100. As he browsed their profiles, though, he was amazed at what he saw. Some of the more outgoing and wild kids had profiles that were kind of boring. But many of the quiet, "good" kids were actually bold in sharing their love of alcohol, unprotected sex, and profanity.

After seeing this, Scott went to his youth pastor with an honest question: "Do the parents of the kids in our youth group really know how their kids act when they're on MySpace?" Scott's pastor knew that the best way to answer that question was with a visual demonstration.

NIGHT OF RECKONING
With Scott's help, his pastor organized a "Parents' Internet Information Night" for the families of all the kids in the junior

---

Rewards for Finding Good Sites

Much of the talk surrounding Internet safety centers on cautioning kids from making online mistakes. So why not accentuate the positive every now and then? Reward your kids when they discover new Internet sites designed to help rather than harm. This does not mean they have carte blanche to surf the Web at will in search of these URLs. But as long as they're following the house rules for Internet safety, be sure to give credit where and when credit is due in this area!

---

high group. Scott created a PowerPoint presentation based on a selection of what he had seen on the MySpace profiles of every kid in the group. He didn't include any specific names, but let the blogs, profile descriptions, pictures, music, and videos from each profile do the talking.

As expected, many of the parents were horrified at what they saw. For every profile that featured uplifting and encouraging poetry, music, and photos, there were five others filled with profanity and pornographic images. After the presentation, the youth pastor spoke to the parents about what motivates "good" kids from respectable families to act out in ways like what they had just seen. He also announced that the church would be setting up a MySpace profile of its own for the junior high group, so the kids would have a place to blog, post pictures, and express themselves in other ways in an environment that had more parental control.

NOT ALL BAD

We've spent much of this book warning you about the dangers of the Internet, not because we love being the bearers of bad news, but because we figured that some readers would be just like we were before we wrote this book—astute enough to have heard the Internet horror stories, but naive enough to think the chances of those things happening to our kids were next to none. Our hope is that we've since changed your mind, educated you, or at least inspired you to delve deeper into your kids' online culture.

Yet for all the real-life dangers opening the door to the Web can invite, let us not forget what positive guests have already shown up at this party. There are many beneficial sites, and the Internet as a whole has much to offer. And though we've given glimpses of that through the previous chapters, let's take a full-fledged dive into some of the wonderful ways the online world can improve life.

Your Family History-dot-com

If you're looking for a fun family project that combines your desire for quality time with your kids and their fascination with the Internet, consider creating a family Web site complete with genealogy researched exclusively online. There are many resources available to help you set up your own site (many of the materials are available without cost). In addition to the treasure hunt experience of discovering relatives you never knew you had, you just may find your own Internet proficiency improving in the process!

ONLINE CONNECTION

With all the focus we've given MySpace in these pages—and for good reason—parents should be aware of a few other social networking sites that, for the most part, have remained clear of such predatory associations.

One of those sites is Classmates.com. Launched in 1995, the site has helped millions of former school pals reconnect, touching countless hearts and families in the process—possibly even yours. The idea is simple: Think of it as an online yearbook for every high school in the United States and Canada. Users register without cost, entering their name, the name of their high school or schools, and the years they attended and graduated. Their information is then entered into the Classmates.com database, which recently passed the forty million mark in registered account holders. Among this extensive catalog of names, members can browse and search for former classmates of their graduating class in hopes of reconnecting. There are also member upgrades available (for a fee) that include such privileges as sending direct e-mail with photos to fellow classmates.[1]

What Classmates.com has done for high school reunions, Match.com has done for the dating industry. In 2004, the matchmaking site entered *Guinness World Records* as the largest online dating service in the world. At that time, more than forty-two million single adults worldwide had registered with Match.com, with more than fifteen million of those actively using the service.[2]

Also worth noting is Dr. Neil Clark Warren's eHarmony.com, which came along five years after the start of Match.com and has made a significant influence in the online singles community. The eHarmony concept starts with an in-depth, 436-item personality profile that covers a variety of different personality "dimensions." Thirteen million single adults are currently members of eHarmony.com, yet the marriage-oriented company is likely most proud of the thousands of eHarmony members who have relinquished their memberships due to tying the knot.[3]

Indeed, not all MySpace experiences are bad. In fact, amidst all the negative stories of MySpace-related crimes, the SNS has had its share of positive reports. In mid-2006, local law enforcement was able to prevent a shooting rampage at a Kansas high school using MySpace. Five teenage boys were accused of planning to initiate a copycat crime on the anniversary of the massacre at Columbine High School, but authorities were alerted when a threatening message was posted on the Web site warning of a potentially deadly attack.

TOOLS GALORE

The Internet's origins were based not on tween-typical talk of cute boys and shopping-mall sales, but instead useful communication between college campuses. To this regard, the Web has not lost its functional basis. Among the millions of useful resources are educational sites, historical pages, dictionaries, almanacs, and various other learning tools. Universities now offer legitimate online courses over the Internet. Government agencies provide key documents and forms online free of charge. Federal and state taxes can be completed and filed without a single sheet of paper being sent. Mapquest.com and similar sites have become savior sites for the directionless among us. And Google—that multifaceted mother of a site—now lets you check out what your childhood home currently looks like . . . from thousands of miles away in outer space. Google Earth offers satellite pictures of virtually every neighborhood (and yes, you can zoom in).

There are also countless admirable organizations that have used the Web simply as an extension of their services, or at least to promote those services. Among those is the United States Marines, which has gotten into the social networking act by setting up a MySpace profile as a recruiting device. Those browsing the page can watch streaming videos of boot camp recruits responding to the orders of barking drill sergeants, as well as Marines storming beaches.

The military likes the fact that it can show teens and young adults a live-action depiction of what it has to offer. And so far, the MySpace crowd is responding. The Marines claim more than 12,000 online friends, a few hundred of whom have gone so far as to click the "Contact a Recruiter" icon.

While the Marines further their SNS presence, America Online hopes to honor the brave soldiers by offering subscribers

---

Connecting with Lost Family

Now that you're equipped and primed to venture across the vast landscape of the Web, use some of these positive tools for good. Search out at least one "lost" family member or friend online during the next year, and then attempt to reconnect with him or her.

who have served in the military the opportunity to reconnect with missing family members. Veterans and family members from any service branch or military can take part in this endeavor. Their online G.I. Photo Library displays pictures of the missing family members, while the online Veterans and Active-Duty Registry displays "Looking for . . ." messages as well. So far the families of more than fourteen and a half million veterans and active-duty members of the armed forces have registered to take part in this service.[4]

Even without a history of military service, you can use the Internet to reconnect with long-lost family members, or even connect with relatives you never knew existed! MyFamily.com is the largest for-profit genealogy company in the world. As a hub of sites devoted to ancestry and family history, its network includes Ancestry.com, FamilyHeritage.com, FamilyTree Maker.com, and Genealogy.com.

The MyFamily.com group features a database with literally billions of registrants (Ancestry.com features more than five billion records online alone, with more added daily). Countless families have been able to trace their family histories through this comprehensive and informative Web site.[5]

And if connecting with family members brings a smile to your face, you can express that joy with the granddaddy of all IM and e-mail accessories: the *buddy icon*! J Web sites like www.OriginalIcons.com give IMers and e-mailers "iconage" to accentuate their communiqués. OriginalIcons.com offers users more than 50,000 different icons to choose from. (Even if you've never ventured into the icon arena as a user, there's a good chance an icon at the end of an e-mail from a friend has brought a smile to your face a time or two!)

LONG TIME COMING

At its worst, the Internet connects its users to harmful ideas, images, and people. But at its best, it remains a tool for recon-

Pushing the Positive

If your kids have discovered the ultimate Web site for icons, they're going to want to "push" that site to their friends. Encourage that! The more they get in the habit of promoting decent and helpful online information, the easier it will be for them to stay in that habit.

necting people who have the most invested in a relationship.

In 1991, Stephanie Lovatos' two-year-old daughter, Celine Aquirei, disappeared with Stephanie's then-boyfriend, who was also Celine's father. Stephanie never gave up searching for her daughter, but after fifteen years of looking, she was beginning to wonder if she'd ever hold her again. Thanks to the Internet, that dream for a reunion turned into reality.

Celine had grown up with her dad and his girlfriend, a woman Celine's father had always told her was her mom. When Celine was thirteen, however, she saw a copy of her own birth certificate for the first time and learned the truth about her biological mother. Despite both mother and daughter now knowing the facts about their relationship, neither really had any idea about how to find the other. Celine had been away from her mom so long, Stephanie's custodial rights would be difficult to enforce. All either one of them could do was to hope and pray for a miracle. That is, until the day Stephanie got an idea: Why not use the computer?

She had heard about MySpace and thought that might be a place where Celine would hang out online. So Stephanie asked a friend to create a MySpace profile for her. In the area asking the question, "Whom would you most like to meet?" Stephanie wrote Celine's name, adding, "I have not seen you since you were two. I have been looking for you all this time. Get ahold of me. I have important information to tell you."

Four months after creating her profile, Stephanie heard from a long-lost cousin, who told her how to use the search function on MySpace. Within minutes, Stephanie found her daughter's profile online—which is where the miraculous enters this story.

It turns out that Celine didn't even use MySpace account; her boyfriend had set it up for her just so she could have one. His thoughtful gesture gave Celine a gift she never could have ever imagined getting: a restored relationship with her mother. In June 2006—fifteen years after their separation—Stephanie and Celine finally met again.[6]

WEB KINDNESS

If you spend your days looking for helpful resources online, chances are you're going to find them. But don't stop there. Use your new discovery for something greater than yourself.

It's amazing how much good can be done with a computer, a modem, and a credit card aimed in the right direction. We are a part of one of the most charitable societies in recent memory. The outpouring of tangible expressions of financial support in

---

Online Missions Project
Select an organization or cause your entire family can support, and then support that exclusively online. Using a combination of e-mail blasts and posts to your own family's or company's Web site, let others know of your cause and offer them the chance to make a financial contribution online.

---

the aftermath of tragedies like the 9/11 attacks and Hurricane Katrina bear testimony to that fact. With the worldwide scope of the Internet, all it takes is a couple of clicks to connect with ministries, non-profit organizations, and international agencies that can put hands and feet to your potential contribution. If you have a compassionate heart and the means to give, don't let a lack of time or the necessary skills keep you from changing the world one life at a time—starting with your own children as they watch you supporting others.

A FAMILY FUNCTION

From sports and entertainment trivia about your favorite performers to discovering new and interesting places to travel—and then booking your accommodations on the spot—the Internet is improving the efficiency of the way we run our lives in so many ways. Consumers are paying their bills online, and even earning legitimate wages via the Internet. By and large, it can be a great place for commerce, communication, and connection. These are important realities to keep in mind when you're determining what kind of Internet usage agreement is best for your family.

It can't be stressed enough that the Internet is not evil in and of itself. But the fact that it's not entirely bad doesn't make it "all good" either. That means it's your job as a parent to make sure that your kids learn how to make the *most* out of their Internet time. Otherwise, it could wind up getting the *best* of them!

Internet Protect Your Kids through the Use of Positive Web sites by:

1. Rewarding your kids when they discover new sites designed to help rather than harm.
2. Establishing a family Web site, complete with genealogy researched exclusively online.
3. Encouraging them to only promote (or "push") positive Web sites to their online friends.
4. Searching out at least one "lost" family member or friend online during the next year and then reconnecting with him or her.
5. Engaging in some sort of philanthropic volunteer activity exclusively online.

EPILOGUE

Sara was in her room later that evening when she heard the knock at the door. A brief conversation followed, the voices so muffled she couldn't understand what was being said. But she knew things weren't going to go well for her when she heard her father call, "Sara, get down here *now!*"

Sara was startled when she walked into the living room downstairs and saw the man from the park sitting on the couch. After a deep sigh, Sara's father spoke.

"Sit down, Sara. This man just told me a most interesting story, and it's about *you.*"

About *her?* Before spotting him at the park, Sara had never seen this man before in her life! What could *he* know about *her?* She was almost too frightened to listen as he began to speak.

"Sara, do you know who I am?"

"Well, no," Sara answered.

"I'm your online friend, 'TheMan23.'"

"No way!"

"Yes, it's true," the man replied.

"'TheMan23' is in high school," Sara confidently stated. "He lives in Nevada. I've seen his profile."

"Actually, you saw a profile of someone who doesn't exist. I'm a police officer, Sara. I created the profile as a decoy."

"But why?" Sara wondered.

"Because there are people online who want to hurt kids like you. I belong to a group of law-enforcement agents who set up these false profiles to help educate children about the dangers of sexual predators online. Too many kids give out way too much information about themselves over the Internet, Sara. That's how I found you."

"What do you mean?"

"You told me where you went to school, what soccer team you played for, where they practiced, when your next game was going to be. You also told me exactly when you would be online every day. Actually, I was just telling your parents how sorry I was that you made it so easy for me to find you."

Sara was silent for just a moment. The shock of the police officer's revelation still hadn't quite worn off yet. When it did, Sara finally spoke up.

"So . . . does that mean you don't live in Las Vegas?"

"No," the officer laughed. "I live a couple miles from here. Did it make you feel safer when you talked to me thinking I lived in another state?"

"Yeah," Sara shrugged. At that moment, the hurt, shame, guilt, and embarrassment finally got to her and she started to sob. Through her tears, she asked the officer, "How many other kids like me have you done this to?"

"More than I'd care to admit," the officer replied. "But I don't mind if you're a little mad at me right now. A buddy of mine had a daughter who was a lot like you. She met some guy online who she thought was about her age, but when she met him, he turned out to be a sexual predator. He convinced her that they should meet one day, and once he got her alone, he killed her.

"We try so hard to teach kids not to talk about personal things with online friends that they've never actually met," he continued. "But so many kids just get careless. Look at you and me. We had only been chatting online a couple of times and you told me lots of personal things about your life and family."

"Yeah, you tricked me," she said angrily.

"You're right," the officer replied. "But sexual predators are *not* going to be honest with you. You have to be ready for that."

Sara got the message that day. She learned a valuable lesson about Internet safety from an adult who cared enough to teach it to her.

A MARATHON, NOT A SPRINT

You have the same opportunity with your own kids. Even if you've never had a talk with your son or daughter about Internet safety before. Even if you don't feel qualified to have that discussion. Make the effort. Your kids are counting on you. Today is the day to start the conversation with your children about Internet safety.

A story is told about a reporter at the 1968 Summer Olympic Games in Mexico City who was getting ready to file his final report after the completion of the marathon, traditionally the final event of the competition.

There were only a handful of people in the stadium now, mostly cleanup crew along with a few other journalists preparing to head back to their home countries. As the reporter packed up his notes and began to leave the stadium, he heard a noise in the distance. Buh-bump . . . buh-bump. The noise grew louder with each buh-bump, so the reporter turned to see what was causing it. At that moment, he saw a weary runner near exhaustion entering the stadium.

His entry number was still pinned to his sweat-soaked tank top. The buh-bump sound he made was the result of a pronounced limp, no doubt caused by an injury sustained while running the race. But now the marathoner had circled the track and crossed the finish line, well behind all the runners who had completed the race before him.

Curiously, the reporter ventured over to where the gimpy athlete was now stooped, bent over forward, hands on his knees, trying to reclaim his breath.

"Do you have any idea what time it is?" the reporter wondered. "The race ended *hours* ago."

"I know," the runner replied between gasps, still staring down at his blistered feet.

"All of the race officials have gone home," the reporter continued. "There won't even be any record of you finishing the race. So why didn't you just quit?"

The runner slowly regained an upright posture and sighed before clearing his throat. "Sir," he responded, "the government and the people of my country invested a lot of money so that I could travel 5,000 miles to compete in this event. They didn't send me here to *start* the race—they sent me here to *finish it.*"[1]

Parenting is not a sprint. It's really more of a marathon. And the reality is, the only preparation most of us receive for this race is the knowledge of where to buy stylish running shoes.

The fact that you chose to read this book is an indication that you're probably already doing a great job parenting the kids God has entrusted to you. Don't let your anxieties about the Internet knock you off course. None of us could have ever imagined even ten years ago that our kids would be spending so much time in this alternate universe online. Like most parents, your parenting plan probably did *not* include a section on how to handle the Internet. That means you're going to need to make some adjustments sooner than later—and that's not always an easy thing to do.

At least a marathon runner *knows* that the race lasts for twenty-six miles and 385 yards, and that he's going to feel like he hit a wall right around mile marker nineteen. Dealing with Internet usage in your home may feel like a wall you can't seem to get around, over, under, or through right now. But the reality is, you *can*. If your children are fairly young at present, you have an excellent chance of being able to "hang" with them as they learn how to maneuver on the Internet. You can keep pace with their online activities. If you have middle school or high school kids at home, you're going to have to work much harder . . . but you *can* still get up to speed.

Start by paying more attention to what your kids are doing online. And build that support system of other parents you can lean on while you learn all you can about the Internet.

Deepening the connection you have with your kids will empower them to make right and wise decisions online and in real life.

Be the parent. Make the investment. Stay the course. *Internet Protect Your Kids.*

APPENDIX A

Sample Internet Usage Agreement

The media have a tremendous influence on kids, especially in the area of Internet use. What they see, hear, and read online often shapes behavior patterns in kids and young adults, but not always for the better. So what can we, as parents, do about monitoring how influential these outside forces will be in the lives of our children?

A verbal arrangement can be relatively easy to manipulate, maneuver around, or break altogether. That's why we recommend establishing firm boundaries in these key areas, and then putting them in *writing*.

The following is a sample of a basic Internet Usage Agreement. Use it as is or as a template of sorts for creating your own. Either way, you'll have a printed standard by which each member of the family can agree on spelling out the terms and conditions under which the Internet can be accessed in your home.

NOTE: Be sure to include each member of the family in the drafting of this document, *especially* your kids. Children are more likely to support the things they help create, so give them every opportunity possible to take ownership of this agreement. It will be much easier to enforce in the long run.

Internet Usage Agreement

- The average amount of time I will spend online will be no more than _____ hours per day.
- I will limit my Web surfing to educational, Christian, or other family-friendly sites only.
- Unsolicited e-mail and forwards with attachments will be deleted unopened.
- Internet filters will be used at all times.
- Mom and Dad have the ultimate veto power over any part of my social networking profile. The first time any part of my profile is deemed inappropriate, the offending item will be deleted. The second time inappropriate material is discovered, the entire profile will be deleted.
- Mom and Dad may authorize an inspection of my instant messenger address book and/or my friends lists on MySpace, Xanga, or any other SNS I use. They may do so for any reason with twenty-four [or twelve or six] hours' advance notice.

_____

[Child's signature and date]

_____

[Parents' signatures and date]

APPENDIX B

SAFE SOCIAL NETWORKING: MYSPACE SAFETY TIPS

As part of their efforts to make MySpace more user-friendly, the operators of this social networking site post the following safety tips online. This first group of instructions is for the users of MySpace (most of whom are primarily high school and middle school age):

MySpace makes it easy to express yourself, connect with friends, and make new ones, but please remember that what you post publicly could embarrass you or expose you to danger. Here are some common sense guidelines that you should follow when using MySpace:

- **Don't forget that your profile and MySpace forums are public spaces.** Don't post anything you wouldn't want the world to know (e.g., your phone number, address, IM screens name, or specific whereabouts). Avoid posting anything that would make it easy for a stranger to find you, such as where you hang out every day after school.

- **People aren't always who they say they are. Be careful about adding strangers to your friends list.** It's fun to connect with new MySpace friends from all over the world, but avoid meeting people in person whom you do not fully know. If you must meet someone, do it in a public place and bring a friend or trusted adult.

- **Harassment, hate speech, and inappropriate content should be reported.** If you feel someone's behavior is inappropriate, react. Talk with a trusted adult, or report it to MySpace or the authorities.

- **Don't post anything that would embarrass you later.** Think twice before posting a photo or info you wouldn't want your parents or boss to see!

- **Don't mislead people into thinking that you're older or younger.** If you lie about your age, MySpace will delete your profile."

In an effort to keep parents better informed about both the benefits and potential hazards of MySpace, the following information is also offered to parents on the "Safety Tips" part of the site:

For teens, MySpace is a popular online hangout because the site makes it easy for them to express themselves and keep in touch with their friends.

As a parent, please consider the following guidelines to help your children make safe decisions about using online communities.

- **Talk to your kids about why they use MySpace, how they communicate with others, and how they represent themselves on MySpace.**

- **Kids shouldn't lie about how old they are. MySpace members must be fourteen years of age or older.** We take extra precautions to protect our younger members, and we are not able to do so if they do not identify themselves as such. MySpace will delete users whom we find to be younger than fourteen, or those misrepresenting their age.

- **MySpace is a public space.** Members shouldn't post anything they wouldn't want the world to know (e.g., phone number, address, IM screen name, or specific whereabouts). Tell your children they should avoid posting anything that would make it easy for a stranger to find them, such as their local hangouts.

- **Remind them not to post anything that could embarrass them later or expose them to danger.** Although MySpace is public, teens sometimes think that adults can't see what they post. Tell them that they shouldn't post photos or info they wouldn't want adults to see.

- **People aren't always who they say they are. Ask your children to be careful about adding strangers to their friends list.** It's fun to connect with new MySpace friends from all over the world, but members should be cautious when communicating with people they don't know. They should talk to you if they want to meet an online friend in person, and if you think it's safe, any meeting should take place in public and with friends or a trusted adult present.

- **Harassment, hate speech, and inappropriate content should be reported.** If your kids encounter inappropriate behavior, let them know that they can let you know, or they should report it to MySpace or the authorities.

APPENDIX C

EXTREME MEASURES: DELETING YOUR CHILD'S MYSPACE PROFILE

There are a number of reasons why a parent would feel it necessary to delete his or her child's MySpace profile. They include but are not limited to:

- The child is under fourteen years of age.
- The family's Internet Usage Agreement does not provide for the use of any social networking sites.
- The child has repeatedly violated the family's Internet Usage Agreement.

You'll find the procedure for removing a child's (or any other user's) MySpace profile in the "FAQ" (Frequently Asked Questions) link from the home page. If you discover that your child has established a MySpace profile without your knowledge, you'll need to work with him to complete the removal process.

1. Log onto MySpace.com and click "Account Settings."
2. Then click "Cancel Account." An e-mail will be sent to the e-mail address that was used to establish the account (which is also the same address you just used to log in).
3. You will receive an "Account Deletion" e-mail from MySpace to verify that the profile has been deleted.

Occasionally the confirmation e-mail will not arrive. *The most common reason this happens is that the e-mail account used to establish the MySpace profile is no longer active.* If your family has switched Internet service providers since your child's

MySpace profile was established, you will not be able to use the removal process listed above.

In the event that your confirmation e-mail does not arrive (regardless of the reason), there is an alternate way to delete the profile.

1. Remove all content from your child's profile.

2. Locate the "About Me" section of the profile and enter in the words "Remove Profile." (This will alert the staff at MySpace that you have taken over your child's profile.)

3. Locate the "Contact MySpace" icon at the bottom of the Web page and send an e-mail to MySpace with the URL to the profile in question (this is the long "techie" address you see on your Web browser's address bar). The MySpace staff will then remove the profile for you.

APPENDIX D

OTHER SOCIAL NETWORKING SITES

MySpace certainly isn't the only social networking site, just the most popular in the United States. Banning your children from using is one solution for keeping them safe from sexual predators and other Internet dangers. But there are countless other social networking sites online, and there's a good chance your kids might shift to one of them if their MySpace or Xanga privileges are revoked.

Here is a partial listing of some of the more widely used social networking sites. Note that many of them are more popular overseas than in the U.S., which might make them seem more attractive to a child who wants to use an SNS without constant grief from her parents.

SITE	TARGET AUDIENCE	NUMBER OF USERS
Facebook	American college students	7.5 million
Faceparty	British teens and twentysomethings	5.7 million
Friendster	Ages eighteen and up	30 million
Hi5	Popular in Europe and Latin America	60 million
LiveJournal	Bloggers and those who like to network	9 million
Mixi	Popular primarily in Japan	3 million
myYearbook	American teenagers	6 million
orkutTeens	(Google's answer to MySpace)	12 million
Tagged	Teens	1 million
Yahoo!	360Social networking arm of Yahoo!	2 million[1]

APPENDIX E

CRACKING THE INSTANT MESSENGER CODE

There are literally thousands of instant message acronyms that kids use when they IM each other. Some of these same abbreviations are also used in e-mail as well. Many of these are harmless and fun. In fact, you may have used a couple of them a time or two when corresponding electronically with friends or workplace colleagues. However, more than a few of these are commonly used by kids as code to keep their parents from figuring out what the *real* topic of their online conversation truly is.

- **aka** (also known as)
- **bak** (back at keyboard)
- **bbl** (be back later)
- **b4n** (bye for now)
- **bf** (boyfriend)
- **bff** (best friend forever/best friends forever)
- **brb** (be right back)
- **fwiw** (for what it's worth)
- **fyi** (for your information)
- **gf** (girlfriend)
- **ggb** (gotta go, bye)
- **g2g** or **gtg** (got to go)
- **idk** (I don't know)
- **imo** (in my opinion)
- **imho** (in my humble opinion)
- **kit** (keep in touch)
- **lmao** (laughing my a— off)
- **lol** (laugh out loud/laughing out loud)
- **ns** (no s—)
- **pls** (please)
- **pos** (parents over shoulder—change subject)

- **rotfl** (rolling on the floor laughing)
- **stfu** (shut the f— up)
- **tmi** (too much information)
- **ttfn** (ta-ta for now)
- **ttyl** (talk to ya later)
- **ttys** (talk to you soon)
- **tx** or **thx** (thanks)
- **uw** (you wish)
- **wtf** (what the f—)

APPENDIX F

ADDITIONAL ONLINE RESOURCES

RECOMMENDED WEB FILTERS AND SPAM BLOCKERS:
- ContentProtect
- CYBERsitter
- Net Nanny
- CyberPatrol
- FilterPak
- Cyber Sentinel
- McAfee Parental Controls
- Norton Parental Controls
- Cyber Snoop
- ChildSafe

RESOURCES FOR HELPING YOUR KIDS DEAL WITH AN ONLINE BULLY:
- WiredSafety.org
- Cyberbully.org
- BullyOnLine.org
- WiredKids.org

RESOURCES FOR DEALING WITH SEXUAL PREDATORS
- WiredSafety.org
- NetSmartz.org
- SexualOffenders.com
- NationalAlertRegister.com

SUGGESTED SITES FOR MORE ONLINE SAFETY PRODUCTS:
- CommonSenseMedia.org
- WebWiseKids.org
- SafeTeens.com

- GetNetWise.com
- iSafe.org
- BlogSafety.com
- Software4Parents.com
- SafeEyes.com

ENDNOTES

Chapter 1

1. Pew Internet and American Life Project, "Teens and Technology," July 27, 2005, http://www.pewinternet.org/pdfs/PIP_Teens_Tech_July 2005web.pdf.
2. Jerry Ropelato, "Internet Pornography Statistics," *TopTenReviews*, August 28, 2006, http://internet-filter-review.toptenreviews.com/internet-pornography-statistics.html.
3. Janis Wolak, et al., National Center for Missing & Exploited Children, "Online Victimization of Youth: Five Years Later," 2006,http://www.missingkids.com/en_US/publications/NC167.pdf.
4. Pew, "Teens and Technology."
5. Ibid.

Chapter 2

1. Mark Hachman, "House Bill Seeks to Ban Teens from Social Networking Sites," May 15, 2006, http://www.foxnews.com/story/0,2933,195270,00.html.
2. The Kaiser Family Foundation, "Generation M: Media in the Lives of 8-18 Year-olds," March 9, 2005, http://www.kff.org/entmedia/7251.cfm.

Chapter 3

1. Julie Rawe, "How Safe is MySpace?" *Time*, July 3, 2006, 35.
2. Wolak, "Online Victimization of Youth: Five Years Later."
3. "Cbyer911 Emergency," August 31, 2006, http://wiredsafety.org/cyberstalking_harassment/csh2.html.

Chapter 4

1. Ropelato, "Internet Pornography Statistics."
2. Ibid.
3. Ibid.

4. Ibid.

5. Ibid.

6. Jerry Ropelato, "P2P Networking–Kids Know! Do Mom and Dad?" *TopTenReviews*, August 28, 2006, http://internet-filter-review.toptenreviews.com/peer-to-peer-file-sharing.html.

7. Ibid.

8. Ibid.

9. Antone Gonsalves, "Three of Four U.S. Homes Have Broadband," June 22, 2006, http://www.techweb.com/wire/ebiz/189600680.

10. For a detailed story, check out http://www.oprah.com/tows/pastshows/200602/tows_past_20060215.jhtml

Chapter 5

1. Spencer Reiss, "His Space," *Wired*, July 2006, 164.

2. Pew, "Teens and Technology."

3. Patricia Odell, "Live from Ad:Tech: According to Kids Online," *Promo*, November 9, 2005, http://promomagazine.com/news/adtech_kidsonline_110905.

4. Stephen Arterburn and Jim Burns, *Parents Guide to Top 10 Dangers Teens Face* (Colorado Springs: Tyndale, 1995), 69.

5. Viv Groskop, "Internet Killed the Video Star," *New Statesman*, July 10, 2006, http://www.newstatesman.com/200607100034.

6. Nielsen/NetRatings, "Kids and Teens Spending More Time Online Than Ever Before," Oct. 11, 2006, http://www.nielsen-netratings.com/pr/pr_061011.pdf.

7. *Burst Media Online Insights* 6, No. 4 (2006), http://www.burstmedia.com/assets/newsletter/items/2006_05_01.pdf.

8. Pew, "Teens and Technology."

9. Pew Internet and American Life Project, "Cell Phone Study," April 4, 2006, http://www.pewinternet.org/pdfs/PIP_Cell_Phone_Study.pdf.

Chapter 6

1. Hayley DiMarco, as told to Jim Burns on the *HomeWord* radio program, "Dealing with the 'Mean Girls' in Your Life (Part 1)," April 25, 2005.
2. http://www.ryanpatrickhalligan.com.
3. Bob Sullivan, "Cyberbullying Newest Threat to Kids," August 9,2006, http://www.msnbc.msn.com/id/14272228.
4. Al Tompkins, "Viral Videos," *Al's Morning Meeting*, June 29, 2006, http://poynter.org/column.asp?id=2&aid=103841.

Chapter 7

1. Rachel Rosmarin, "Internet Karaoke Gets Serious," *Forbes*, August 4, 2006, http://www.msnbc.msn.com/id/14142291/.
2. The term "consumer sex" is taken from Dr. Jennifer Roback Morse, *Smart Sex: Finding Life-Long Love in a Hook-Up World* (Dallas: Spence Publishing, 2005), 61.
3. Data collected from www.MySpace.com, August 7, 2006.
4. The Barna Group, "Church Attendance," http://www.barna .org/FlexPage.aspx?Page=Topic&TopicID=10.
5. The Barna Group, "Most Twentysomethings Put Christianity on the Shelf Following Spiritually Active Teen Years," September 11, 2006, http://www.barna.org/FlexPage.aspx?Page=Barna Update&BarnaUpdateID=245.
6. Hugh Hewitt, from the radio program *HomeWord with Jim Burns*, "Blogging for Dummies (Part 1)," March 21, 2006.
7. Enid Burns, "Global VoIP Market Takes Hold," August 24, 2006, http://www.clickz.com/showPage.html?page=3623253.

Chapter 8

1. Special thanks to Christian radio programmer and consultant Matt Williams for introducing me to the concept of the "push/pull" nature of the Internet.
2. Leslie Cyester, RN, BSN, and Kathy W. Michael, *The MySpace DeGeneration* (2005–2006), 11.

3. Anick Jesdanun, "Youths No Longer Predominant at MySpace," October 5, 2006, http://www.foxnews.com/wires/2006Oct05/0,4670,SocialNetworkingYouths,00.html.

4. Gary Chapman and Ross Campbell, M.D., *The Five Love Languages of Children* (Chicago: Moody Press, 1997).

5. Associated Press, "Study: Female Chat-Room Names Generate More Threats," May 12, 2006, http://www.foxnews.com/story/0,2933,195293,00.html.

Chapter 9

1. Reuters, "CinemaNow Unveils Download-to-Burn Movie Service," July 20, 2006, http://www.foxnews.com/story/0,2933,204376,00.html.

2. Michael Medved, as told to the National Religious Broadcasters breakfast at the 1996 National Association of Broadcasters Convention, Las Vegas, Nevada.

3. Enid Burns, "Marketing Opportunities Emerge in Online Gaming Venues," August 2, 2006, http://www.clickz.com/showPage.html?page=3623035.

4. Ibid.

5. BBC News, "Cash Card Taps Virtual Game Funds" May 2, 2006, http://news.bbc.co.uk/2/hi/technology/4953620.stm.

6. Olivia and Kurt Bruner, *Playstation Nation: Protect Your Child from Video Game Addiction* (New York: Center Street, a division of Hachette Book Group, 2006), 51.

7. AOL-AP Games Poll, "Survey: Four in 10 American Adults Play Video Games," May 9, 2006, http://www.foxnews.com/story/0,2933,194659,00.html.

8. Ibid.

9. Jim Burns, *The 10 Building Blocks for a Happy Family* (Ventura, CA: Regal Books, 2003), 138.

Chapter 10

1. Brian Bergstein, "Wikipedia Founder Wants Better Site,"

August 4, 2006, http://www.msnbc.msn.com/id/14186665/.

2. Enid Burns, "Wikipedia's Popularity and Traffic Soar," May 10, 2005, http://www.clickz.com/showPage.html?page=3504061.

3. Retrieved from a blog entry from MySpace profile "You Can't Fight the Moonlight," April 19, 2006, http://www.myspace.com.

4. Pew, "Teens and Technology."

5. Center for Parent/Youth Understanding, "Finding Teenagers Online: A Step-by-Step Approach to Navigating Their Online World," http://www.cpyu.org/Page.aspx?id=101385.

6. Retrieved from a blog entry from MySpace profile "Kim," May 18, 2006, http://www.myspace.com.

7. Retrieved from a blog entry from MySpace profile "But why is the rum gone?" March 23, 2006, http://www.myspace.com.

8. Retrieved from a blog entry from MySpace profile "I DON'T KNOW I DON'T KNOW," March 21, 2006, http://www.myspace.com.

9. Mark Henderson, "Scientists: Internet, Chat Rooms Good for Teenagers," *The Times of London*, February 24, 2006, http://www.foxnews.com/story/0,2933,185823,00.html.

10. Hugh Hewitt, *Blog: Understanding the Information Reformation That's Changing Your World* (Nashville: Thomas Nelson, 2005).

11. http://www.marshallmcluhan.com/main.html

Chapter 11

1. http://en.wikipedia.org/wiki/EBay

2. http://en.wikipedia.org/wiki/Google

3. Data collected from www.MySpace.com, August 7, 2006.

Chapter 12

1. Hugh Hewitt, "Blogging for Dummies (Part 1)."

Chapter 13

1. http://en.wikipedia.org/wiki/Classmates.com

2. http://en.wikipedia.org/wiki/Match.com

3. http://business.enotes.com/company-histories/eharmony-com-inc/cupid

4. http://members.aol.com/veterans/warlib15.htm

5. http://en.wikipedia.org/wiki/Myfamily.com

6. "MySpace Enables Mom, Daughter Reunion," July 5, 2006, http://www.cbsnews.com/stories/2006/07/05/earlyshow/main177 5244.shtml

Epilogue

1. As told by Jim Burns on the HomeWord radio program, "A Man's Guide to the Heart of a Woman (Part 2)," September 27, 2006.

Appendices

1.http://en.wikipedia.org/wiki/List_of_social_networking_web sites

NEW LIFE Ministries

Transforming Lives...

...Through God's Truth

New Life Ministries is a non-profit organization, founded by author and speaker, Stephen Arterburn. Our mission is to identify and compassionately respond to the needs of those seeking healing and restoration through God's truth.

New Life's ministry of healing and transformation includes:

- ❧ *New Life Live!* – our daily, call-in counseling radio program hosted by Stephen Arterburn.
- ❧ *Counselors* – our network of over 700 counsleors nationwide. Call 1-800-New-Life to find one near you.
- ❧ *Workshops and conferences*
  - *Every Man's Battle*
  - *Healing is a Choice*
  - *Lose It For Life*
  - *Relationships Reframed*
  - *Every Heart Restored*
  - *Nights of Healing*
- ❧ *Coaching* – Our personal coaching program is "Professional Accountability" to come alongside you and give you solution-focused direction.
- ❧ *Website*
  - podcasts and broadcasts of *New Life Live!*
  - blogs, message boards and chats
  - our online store, featuring products by our radio show hosts
  - find workshops and counselors in your area

1-800-New-Life   www.newlife.com

HOME HW WORD

ENCOURAGING PARENTS, BUILDING FAMILIES

Get Equipped with HomeWord...

LISTEN
HomeWord Radio
programs reach over 1000 communities nationwide with *HomeWord with Jim Burns* – a daily ½ hour interview feature, *HomeWord Snapshots* – a daily 1 minute family drama and *HomeWord this Week* – a ½ hour weekend edition of the daily program.

CLICK
HomeWord.com
provides advice and resources to millions of visitors each year. A truly interactive website, HomeWord.com provides access to HW newsletters, Q&A columns, online broadcasts, tip sheets, our online store and more.

READ
HomeWord Resources
equip families and Churches worldwide with practical books, tip sheets and small group curriculum. Many of these resources are also packaged digitally to meet the needs of today's busy parents.

ATTEND
HomeWord Events
Understanding Your Teenager, Building Healthy Morals & Values, Generation 2 Generation and Refreshing Your Marriage are held in over 100 communities nationwide each year. HomeWord events educate and encourage parents while providing answers to life's most pressing parenting and family questions.

A Ministry with *Jim Burns*

In response to the overwhelming needs of parents and families, Jim Burns founded HomeWord in 1985. HomeWord, a Christian organization, equips and encourages parents, families, and churches worldwide.

Find Out More
Sign up for our FREE daily e-devotional and parent e-newsletter at HomeWord.com, or call 800.397.9725.

HomeWord.com

Every Man has Secrets

Whether they are sinful—or simply not in your best inter-
est . . . whether you wall them off or stuff them down
deep, you are not alone. But as author Stephen Arterburn
warns, secrets are also the most dangerous force within
a man, so finding a way to deal with the unspoken fears
and questions that threaten to undo you is among your
most important tasks.

In this book, the author of the million-selling Every Man's

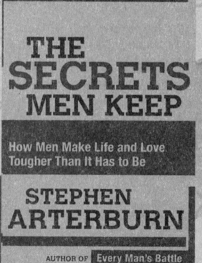

Battle series courageous-
ly exposes what nearly
4,000 men like you said
they think, feel and question—about themselves,
their work, their marriage
and family, their finances
and their faith—but don't
dare to talk about. He also
affirms again and again
that the strength it takes
to keep your secrets safe
can be redirected to make
a better life and a
stronger you.

Throughout these pages, Arterburn not only fleshes out
each of the 25 secrets but gives perspective on where
those secrets come from, why they feel so important and
how to respond to them . . . to make life, work and leadership easier for you and for everyone who loves you.

ISBN-13: 9-781-59145-469-4   **ISBN-10: 1-59145-469-7**
Available wherever books are sold